The Daring Flight of My Pen

Historia de la Nueva Mexico, 1610

Pasó por Aquí Series on the Nuevomexicano Literary Heritage

Edited by

Genaro M. Padilla and A. Gabriel Meléndez

Etching of Gaspar Pérez de Villagrá
in 1610 edition

The Daring Flight of My Pen

Cultural Politics and Gaspar Pérez de Villagrá's
Historia de la Nueva Mexico, 1610

Genaro M. Padilla

UNIVERSITY OF NEW MEXICO PRESS

Albuquerque

© 2010 by Genaro M. Padilla
All rights reserved. Published 2010
Printed in the United States of America

15 14 13 12 11 10   1 2 3 4 5 6

LIBRARY OF CONGRESS CATALOGING-IN-PUBLICATION DATA

Padilla, Genaro M., 1949–
The daring flight of my pen: cultural politics and Gaspar Pérez de Villagrá's Historia de la Nueva Mexico, 1610 / Genaro M. Padilla.
    p. cm.—(Pasó por aquí series on the Nuevomexicano literary heritage)
Includes bibliographical references and index.

ISBN 978-0-8263-4970-5 (cloth: alk. paper)

1. Villagrá, Gaspar Pérez de, d. 1620. Historia de la Nueva México.
I. Title.

PQ7296.V54H577 2010
861'.3—dc22
                            2010023141

For my mother, Esperanza, and in
memory of my father, Manuel

Contents

FOREWORD
ix

ACKNOWLEDGMENTS
xiii

PROLOGUE
1

CHAPTER 1
FABLES OF LA NUEVA MÉXICO
11

CHAPTER 2
LA COLONIA: THE UNSETTLED FIRST SETTLEMENT
43

CHAPTER 3
ACOMA: EL PEÑOL ENSANGRADO
83

EPILOGUE
125

NOTES
131

BIBLIOGRAPHY
145

INDEX
151

Foreword

I am delighted to write the foreword for Genaro Padilla's new book aptly titled *The Daring Flight of My Pen: Cultural Politics and Gaspar Pérez de Villagrá's* Historia de la Nueva Mexico, 1610. In this intellectually engrossing new study of the soldier-poet Gaspar Pérez de Villagrá's epic poem, Padilla does a magnificent job of skillfully analyzing and offering a counterreading of the *Historia de la Nueva Mexico* (1610). In an elegant, probing, highly perceptive and personal style, Padilla undertakes a hermeneutics of the poem's chronicling of the history of the expedition, the conquest, and the colonizing project of New Mexico by Captain Juan de Oñate and his soldiers/colonizers. The author posits a reading of the *Historia* that is quite different and highly original from other works since he does not view Villagrá's epic as one designed solely to honor and glorify the conquistadores. He masterfully teases out how Villagrá's epic poem deconstructs and critiques imperial power through the imaginative juxtaposition of the various documents emerging from the colonization process: native myths, letters, *requerimientos*, creative poetry, theatrical performances, official documents, and in addition, Villagrá's own representation of the events as soldier and an eyewitness participant in the conquest.

Padilla chose a very challenging book to write about—Villagrá's epic poem, a text written in sixteenth-century Spanish—but it is a study that needed to be done. Villagrá's literary oeuvre is very important since it is the first sustained epic poem describing the early European colonization of one of the fifty states in the Union. It is part and parcel of the history of the United States—i.e., the conquest and settlement of the state of New Mexico. In addition, it is the first epic poem written in what is today the United States. Yet, very few scholars tackle this work for various reasons: it is not an easy read, it is written in Spanish, and/or is not perceived as part of United States history and literary production. Padilla manages to offer a brilliant excursion into Villagrá's work while simultaneously doing it in an interesting and readable manner. This is a very enjoyable book to read in spite of the erudition inscribed in the work (frequent classical allusions, sixteen century elegant Spanish, and so forth).

Padilla's scholarship in the hermeneutics of the *Historia* is impeccable. His extensive knowledge of the Greek and Roman classics served him well in his ability to capture the subtle ideological intricacies ensconced in Villagrá's masterpiece. Padilla's familiarity with the Greek and Roman classics is evident in his keen observations regarding the use in the *Historia* of such authors as Homer (*The Odyssey*), Virgil (*Aeneid*), Lucan (*Pharsalia*), Ovid (*Metamorphosis*), Quintilian (*Institutio Oratorio*), Plutarch (*Parallel Lives*), and Livy (*Annals*). Equally important is Padilla's extensive readings of prominent Greek and Roman historical figures as Odysseus, Achilles, Pompey, Sulla, Julius Caesar, Marius, Lucullus, Manilius Imperiosus Torquatus, Seneca, and Aeneas, and his ability to grasp the significant function they play within the Villagrá text. Padilla's intimate knowledge of Greek and Roman classical works aided him greatly in the deconstruction of *La historia de la nueva Mexico*. For example, he was able to detect the connection between Virgil's *Aeneid* and the *Historia* and how Villagrá modeled his own epic poem after it.

Villagrá, however, did not depend solely on the Greek and Roman classics as Padilla accurately informs us, but immersed himself in the Latin American literary epics that were being written in the years before his *Historia*. Of particular importance is Alonso de Ercilla y Zúñiga's epic poem *La Araucana* (published in three parts in 1569, 1578, and 1589), which details with great passion and poetic vigor the resistance of the indigenous population of Chile against the Spanish invaders. Another work influencing Villagrá's work is Bernal Díaz del Castillo *Verdadera historia de la conquista de la Nueva España* (1568) with respect to highlighting the contributions of the common soldier instead of glorifying one man in the imperial project. Padilla also perceives a close connection and intertextuality between Miguel de Cervantes's tragic play *El cerco de Numancia* (1585) and the battle of Acoma in Villagrá's epic.

Padilla posits that in an analogous manner to Ercilla's *La Araucana*, Villagrá assumed the position of a New World criollo; of one born in the Americas of Spanish parents. He could not perceive the world wholly through the imperial lens of a Spanish conquistador but was already immersed in the viewpoint of the Indigenous populations. According to Padilla, Villagrá could not write solely from a Spaniard's perspective. Thus the battle at Acoma or more precisely, the massacre and subsequent horrific events that took place at Acoma, were narrated keeping in mind, to a certain extent, the Native American population and the injustices committed against them. Padilla perceptively examines how Villagrá was able to do this via his poetic imagination and through the Greek and Roman rhetorical strategies he was deploying in order to escape the watchful eye of the Spanish censors.

There are a number of books published on Gaspar Pérez de Villagrá's major work, but these are mainly critical editions. Some of the better known editions of the *Historia de la Nueva Mexico* include Luis González Obregón (1900), Gilberto Espinosa (1933), Mercedes Junquera (1989), Philadelphio Jaramillo (1990), Miguel Encinias, et al. (1992), and Felipe I. Echenique (1993). However, the works cited are editions and are not sustained analysis of the epic poem. One critical work that does stand out for its meticulous scholarship is Manuel Martín-Rodríguez's book, *Gaspar de Villagrá: Legista, soldado y poeta* (2009). Martín-Rodríguez has done an exhaustive and complete study of Villagrá's biography and writings.

What makes Genaro Padilla's work extraordinary and unique, separate from other existing works on Villagrá, is its accessibility to readers and the personal dialogue that he inserts throughout the scholarly study. There is a conversation taking place between Padilla and the *Historia*. Padilla is a native of New Mexico and can trace his ancestors several generations back, perhaps from the 1600s or 1700s. Furthermore, he lived his early formative years in New Mexico near the town of Española and the Santa Fe area; both his close and extended family still make their home in that region. But he has been able to detach himself from the Spanish "fantasy heritage" common in the minds of many New Mexican Hispanics. His keen intellect has allowed him to clearly see the "other side of the conquest," that is, the Native American point of view. He has been able to comprehend the enormity of the injustices committed against the Pueblo Indians by the Spanish conquistadors, who are in part his ancestors. Padilla also traces his genealogy to New Mexican Native Americans and is therefore not of "pure Spanish blood" but a mestizo. This personal dialogue interspersed throughout the scholarly analysis plus the challenging ethical questions posed in the book make it difficult to stop reading. As one leafs through the pages of the book, the reader looks forward to those intimate and heartfelt conversations Padilla carries on with the *Historia*. Villagrá's work comes alive and speaks to us, contemporary readers in our own time and place. The *Historia* is no longer a dusty, long-forgotten, seventeenth-century document but one that speaks to us in the here and now. The blood spilt on the Acoma mesa by the Spanish soldiers continues to fertilize each subsequent generation of indigenous peoples and insures that the crimes visited upon their ancestors are never forgotten.

Genaro Padilla is a gifted storyteller and scholar; his skillful use of the English language is both innovative and creative. His style of writing, both personal and scholarly, is bound to please both specialists of Villagrá's work and beginning students. Readers will find Padilla's book a pleasure to read as well as intellectually rich and rewarding.

—María Herrera-Sobek, University of California–Santa Barbara

Acknowledgments

As with any book project, my study owes a thankful debt to many people who encouraged me, asked difficult questions, read portions, and, in some cases, all of the manuscript, offered commentary and criticism, and in many ways made my work better, I believe, for the challenges they posed.

Indeed, as is often the case with a research project, this book started with a set of questions and concerns about a Spanish colonial epic that I thought would provide material sufficient for a lecture, an essay, perhaps an opening chapter, but which eventually developed into a longer conversation with, and about, an epic poem published exactly four hundred years ago: Gáspar Pérez de Villagrá's *Historia de la Nueva Mexico*. While he was New Mexico state historian, Estevan Rael-Gálvez first invited me to give lectures on my initial readings of the *Historia de la Nueva Mexico* in Taos and Albuquerque in the summer of 2007. Dennis Trujillo, assistant state historian, prompted me to post the lecture on the state historian's website and then edited my first published words on the poem. Manuel M. Martin-Rodríguez, my friend and colleague from University of California, Merced, encouraged my interest in Villagrá over long conversations. It was only after reading his remarkably lucid and rich essays on Villagrá's poem and archive that I was prompted to write something of my own. I completed my manuscript just as the first volume of Manuel's monumental study, *Villagrá: Soldado, Legista, y Poeta* was published in Spain (Universidad de León, 2009); I can't help but know that my work would have been tremendously enriched had I had his book on my desk as I wrote. Gabriel Meléndez let me test portions of chapters in his graduate seminar at the University of New Mexico and offered methodological suggestions for strengthening my reading. I am grateful for his long intellectual and personal friendship. Professor Anne Goldman offered sustained editorial commentary and a critical intelligence that enriched my thinking about epic as a genre of competing rhetorical and ideological forces, all of which eased my trepidation about writing on a colonial text. María Herrera-Sobek and Francisco Lomelí, longtime friends and colleagues, have always encouraged my work, and, indeed, María has written on Villagrá in ways that wonderfully illuminated and further provoked my thinking about the poem. My Berkeley pal Mitchell Breitweiser read drafts of every chapter and offered suggestions, and a cold beer whenever necessary. Professors Jose Davíd Saldívar, Michael Trujillo, Phillip "Felipe" Gonzales, Enrique Lamadrid, great colleagues all, I thank you. Rosa Martinez, my graduate student and research assistant, not only found elusive material, but more importantly enriched my thinking through her own daringly insightful writing on the poem.

Professor Luis Leal is remembered here for his kindness and in no small part for his scholarly trailblazing, which opened space for so many of us to study our long literary heritage—after he had set foot in nearly every direction of that heritage and then beckoned us graciously forward.

The Bancroft Library staff graciously allowed me to study the 1610 edition in the reading room, and then prepared digital images for use in my book. Clark Whitehorn, editor-in-chief at the University of New Mexico Press, has been a friend to this project from its inception, and Meredith Dodge, my copyeditor, helped make every sentence and every paragraph clear and comprehensible.

Finally, my family has always provided the affection and space I need for writing. My wife, María, as usual, let me fill a corner table with books, papers, and various gadgets in order to get this book done; my kids, Andre, Genaro, Jessica, Xochi, and Camila have seen how happy I am to be writing again after "doing administration" and I love them for all for the spirit they bring into my life. My mother, Esperanza "Hope" Padilla, who you will meet in this book, has inspired my research on our culture and literature since I was a child. And then, my bros Alonzo, Lefty, and Eddie listened with "oh yeah?" smiles during our many fishing expeditions along the same rivers where much of the story of Villagrá's *Historia de la Nueva Mexico* took place more than four hundred years ago.

Prologue

The year is 1610.

One of the soldiers who explored and helped colonize the first Spanish settlement in the far northern reaches of empire is scratching out the final stanzas of an epic poem about his exploits that will be published in April under the title *Historia de la Nueva Mexico*. Gaspar Pérez de Villagrá, a criollo born in Puebla de los Ángeles, Mexico, aspires to join the ranks of other soldiers who have turned to the pen to win fame and wealth.

The period around 1610 is an extraordinary moment for art and discovery. As Villagrá is musing over his verse, Galileo Galilei is observing the satellite moons of Jupiter using the revolutionary technology of the telescope, while Johannes Fabricius discovers sunspots. El Greco is painting the *Laocoon* and *The View and Plan of Toledo*, and Peter Paul Rubens is finishing *Philomenes Recognized by the Old Woman* and *The Elevation of the Cross*. Having completed his final paintings, *The Denial of St. Peter* and *David with the Head of Goliath*, Michelangelo Merisi Caravaggio dies of malaria in Tuscany. In Padua, the Academy of Poetry is founded. William Shakespeare composed his three great romances during this period: *Cymbeline, The Winter's Tale*, and *The Tempest*. At theaters closer to the soldier's Spanish home, Lope de Vega's Old Testament drama *La hermosa Ester* and his pastoral *Peribáñez* play to audiences ecstatic for another of the prodigious playwright's dramas.

Across the seas in the New World, Henry Hudson, commissioned to find a northwestern passage to India, sails into an icy, fog-pressed bay that would be renamed in his honor—only long after mutineers set him adrift in a small boat and he was never seen again. At Jamestown, some five hundred English colonists perish during the starving time; the sixty who remain, it is rumored, have survived by cannibalizing their brethren.

PROLOGUE

In August, the English attack the Indian village of Paspahegh, destroy the cornfields, and then execute the queen and her children. The first Spanish settlers in la nueva México, the place Gaspar Pérez de Villagrá traces in his poem, move from their colony in the river valley settlement of San Gabriel to a spot twenty miles south at the foot of the Sangre de Cristo mountain range. Here, under the name La Villa Real de la Santa Fe de San Francisco de Asís, it becomes the capital of what is now New Mexico. We know this small city today as Santa Fe. As Villagrá finishes his epic back in Spain, the Acoma people who survived the slaughter of their pueblo—an attack the writer-soldier himself took part in—complete the tenth year of their servitude to the Spanish, punishment for defending themselves on their mesa home in 1599.

~ 1 ~

Four hundred years later, I wait for the reference librarian in the Bancroft Library at Berkeley to retrieve one of perhaps twelve surviving copies of the *Historia de la Nueva Mexico*. Because one must have permission to handle the book that tells a story in verse of the 1598 Spanish colonial settlement of what is now New Mexico, the librarian suggests I use the microfilm copy and then says, "Of course, there is a digital copy of the original 1610 one can read on the internet from anywhere in the world." I understand. This advice is a crucial strategy for protecting the original edition held in the Bancroft vault. Still, I would like to hold the actual book in my hand, feel its weight and turn its pages, so that I might see what a seventeenth-century reader would have seen. I have read and studied the digital facsimile of Villagrá's poem on the large, bright screen of the computer in the seclusion of my office, drinking coffee as I scroll across the virtual images of this poem published half a world away four centuries ago. The digital facsimile is clear, easy to read, with no pages one must turn carefully—simply touch the "next image" icon and, magic, another page of verse. Nor do I need fret about the protective archival protocols prohibiting bags, purses, and cell phones and permitting only pencils, a single writing pad, or a laptop with which to take notes. Yet, when the librarian conveys the small box containing the original text—*Historia de la Nueva Mexico, Del Capitán Gaspar de Villagrá*—the old-fashioned aura of the archive comes over me, and the digital text evaporates. The original is a small volume, a mere 5⅜ by 3½ inches and just 1 inch thick, yet its materiality is disarming. Looking at this book I realize that all the protocols are necessary. I turn the pages with a care and an affection I do not accord most of the books on my shelves, and it would be horrifying to hold a cup of coffee above the text as I read. Imagining myself as one of Villagrá's original readers, I scan the book's opening lines and hear at once the classical echoes of Homer's immortal epics, Virgil's *Aeneid*, as well as the inflections of Ercilla's *La Araucana* and those other epics and stories of the New World that enticed the Spanish imagination.

Yet in the centuries that have elapsed since its first printing, Gaspar Pérez de Villagrá's *Historia de la Nueva Mexico* appears to have been little read, its pages seldom turned. When it has been read, the poem has been consulted chiefly as a sourcebook by historians writing about the Spanish colonial period of the American Southwest. That is how I was taught to read the *Historia*—a history of New Mexico. Now it is the subject of the book I am finishing in 2010. Now, I am reading it appropriately, as a poem, an epic in which history is made subordinate to its literary imagining.

The original *Historia* in hand, I imagine a scene set more than four hundred years ago. A man—a soldier—his own New World epic in his saddlebag, is riding from Madrid to Alcalá to meet with the owner of a press. The quilled poem is protected in a leather satchel, words scratched out here and there across its pages, meter regularized to hendecasyllabic form, phrasing revisions marked above the penned text, thousands of lines, written over hundreds of days, and as finished as it was likely to get. The soldier has waited many months for the court censors to review and approve his poem,[1] and in late December 1609, the King's seal is at last conferred by Maestro Vicente Espinel: "La historia de la nueva Mexico, poema heroico del Capitán Gaspar de Villagrá, no tiene cosa contra la Fé ni buenas costrumbres."[2] The poem contains nothing of danger to church, society, or the king.

Granted license to proceed, Villagrá is free to meet with Luys Martínez Grande, who operates a printing press in Alcalá and with whom he has presumably arranged publication of the verse narration of his adventure in New Spain as an officer in Juan de Oñate's colonial expedition. Naturally, the two men would have discussed editorial matters like errata policy, compositor pay, plate dimensions, and, of course, they negotiated the final cost of printing, including the king's taxes, in order to set the price per council mandate—133 maravedis per copy. Perhaps Martínez Grande made arrangements for the prefatory verse tributes celebrating Villagrá's heroism and poetic skills, Oñate's leadership, and Castile's imperial power.

PROLOGUE

The nine poems that precede the epic story are the equivalent of the advertising blurbs we see on book jackets today. These *sonetas, décimas,* and *canciones* are intended to read as though offered by acquaintances, but are mainly written by well-regarded poets who likely composed them for small commissions.

After viewing the final plates, perhaps the author and printer dine together and talk into the night about Villagrá's experience in la nueva México, about the vast herds of bison and *los indios* who hunt them, about the market for colonial narratives and epics, and perhaps about that other soldier-writer born in Alcalá, Miguel de Cervantes, whose own book was so recently a sensation. The battle at Acoma—such a prominent part of the poem—might well have come into the conversation. I imagine Martínez Grande asking questions about Villagrá's own part in the battle that this soldier, self-effacing, haltingly answered. Presumably they parted amiably, for a few days later the soldier's poem is transformed from handwritten manuscript to a small octavo text of 287 leaves of verse: 24 unnumbered leaves of prefatory poetry and other front matter and then the epic poem in thirty-four cantos spanning 11,891 unrhymed hendecasyllabic lines.

I imagine the fifty-five-year-old soldier-poet holding the book in his hand at the printer's shop, opening it to the title page where he sees the title and his name, *Historia de la Nueva Mexico, Del Capitán Gaspar de Villagrá*, and then turning the leaf to study his own likeness, the etching of a man's figure in armor and stiff formal collar, stocky and balding, with heavy mustache and goatee, hard wrinkles around his eyes, and two deep lines creasing his brow. "Ay, pero ¡que feo!" he might say with a wince, as most of us do seeing ourselves in contrived and uncomfortable poses. He stands at a window in the printer's shop for a long moment, turning the pages of the poem he has labored over with the audacity all books require of their authors but that, for an old soldier with no record of literary achievement, must be particularly bold. Maestro Vicente Espinel would write that Villagrá was an amateur poet—"el verso es numeroso, y aun que desnudo de invenciones y flores poéticos." Villagrá may well have cringed at Espinel's offhand remark, since this censor's note hangs at the front of the poem. Already anticipating his critics, though, Villagrá has written in the opening canto that his verse, however unskilled ("tosca pluma," 1.13), flows from a soldier's courage: "El atrevido buelo de mi pluma"—"the daring flight of my pen" (1.44). So he must have been appeased by what Espinel offered as explanation—"por ser historia seguida y verdadera la variedad de tan extraordinarios y nuevos sucessos, alentará y dará gusto, a todos géneros de gente." The *Historia* was a "sustained and true" account, full of novel and extraordinary events that would provide pleasure and excitement for all classes of readers. Standing in Martínez Grande's shop, a stack of books on a nearby table, Villagrá must have wagered that the sale of his book would lift his small family to financial well-being. Despite his hopes, the *Historia de la Nueva Mexico* never gained the wide popularity that other New World epic, Alonso de Ercilla's Chilean epic *La Araucana* (1569), enjoyed.[3] And Cervantes's comic knight's tale, *Don Quixote*, already wildly popular in 1610, eclipsed not only Villagrá's heroic poem but also devastated the entire epic genre, so that the copies Villagrá carried away to market disappeared one by one. Fewer than a dozen originals survive today.

One of these rare first editions has made its way to a table in the reading room of the Bancroft Library where I sit today. Over the next few months, I read from a canto here, another there, wondering what Villagrá's first readers must have made of the poem. The narrative evokes scenes of that long journey across the desert and the first crossing of the Rio Grande near present-day El Paso, Texas, the expedition of hundreds of people drawing to a final stop at Ohkay Owingeh, a Tewa village in what is now northern New Mexico. And then, in canto thirty-one, I read these disturbing lines: "No de otra suerte juntos todos vimos, / De subito gran suma de difuntos, / Tullidos, mancos, cojos, destroncados / Abiertos por los pechos, mal heridos." We had "no other choice," the soldier-turned-poet writes, but "to see, all of us, the great heap of dead, the maimed, without hands, lame, their breasts torn open, mortally wounded."[4] The pueblo of Acoma was destroyed, its people massacred. Villagra's images of death, at once an echo of classical epic popular precisely for such gore, are rendered here as a soldier's haunting recollection of the massacre he not only witnessed but also carried out. The poet's scene of devastation prefigures the punitive maiming of the male Acoma and the dispersal of the tribe after the battle. The canto remains silent, however, on the Spanish continuation of the slaughter and burning of the village even after the Acoma had offered to surrender. I stare across the reading room, troubled by Villagrá's simultaneous admission and retraction of guilt.

Late every afternoon, I am asked to return the centuries-old book to the vault, where, I trust, it will remain safe for another four centuries. As I leave the library, I think about the ways this long poem traces a rapacious encounter with native people, an empire's soldier narrating another colonial expedition, yet also traces brutality as it has been repeated from classical to New World epic. As a soldier's story, the *Historia* discloses Villagrá's own complex relation to power, that of the King and the nation. As a poem, the book reveals his moral dilemma over the massacre of hundreds of Acoma people.

~ 2 ~

Gaspar de Villagrá's epic was doomed from the beginning to be read as history rather than poetry. Perhaps it was the title: *Historia de la Nueva Mexico*. Having been a soldier for longer than he had been a poet, Villagrá may not, in fact, have written a masterpiece. Still, he labored to emulate the classics he had loved when he was a student at the Universidad de Salamanca in the early 1570s. Though he read for the law, as part of the wider humanist education required of all university students during the Renaissance, he would have studied the Greek and Roman historians and rhetoricians from whom he absorbed the rhetorical maneuvers of Seneca and Quintilian and the historiographic method of Livy. Along with Homer's books and Virgil's *Aeneid* he of course also read Lucan's *Pharsalia* and Ovid's *Metamorphoses*. His poetry may well have suffered from the chronicle imperative he chose for much of the *Historia*, but when all is said and done, it remains an epic that by its nature required a distinct kind of imagination to write—and to read. Real though his experience was in the late 1590s, he had by 1610 transformed it into an epic narrative fashioned through a mechanics of verse, which, I will argue, subordinates history to the play of language—of metaphor, poetic diction, formal meter, epic simile in the canto openings, and a rich field of intertextual allusion to myth, fable, biblical as well as new world figures, and stories of earlier Spanish exploration in la nueva México. Villagra's *Historia* is built in poetry and hence is a fiction of history.

Despite his labor, however, Villagrá is remembered chiefly as a historian whose verse chronicles a Spanish colonial expedition and settlement. The writer did not help his own cause when in the prologue to the poem he makes explicit his connection with the great Roman historian Livy without naming his greater debt to Virgil, upon whose *Aeneid* his own poem is chiefly modeled. Indeed, though Villagrá narrates the Oñate expedition from its inception in 1595 to the battle at Acoma in 1599, it is to Virgil and the classical epic that his poem owes its ability to fuse the purely imaginative with historical events related by an omniscient narrator who, in Villagrá's case though not in Virgil's, was a participant in the history he reconfigures. As the poet tells his first reader, King Felipe III, "Escúchame, gran Rey, que soi testigo / De todo quanto aquí, señor, os digo"—Hear me, great King, for I am witness / Of all that here, my Lord, I say to you" (1.47–48). Indeed, as the *Historia* unfolds, Villagrá mixes a running chronicle of the journey he took with the figurative language of poetry and a vast inventory of allusion to classical and biblical literature, not to mention the legendry of the pre-Columbian Americas.[5]

In the opening cantos, for example, rather than the Iberian legend a Spaniard might be expected to relate, Villagrá recreates the Aztec myth of origin in the far northern reaches of empire. Unlike Camões's *Os Lusiadas* (1572), which charts Vasco de Gama's voyage to India and synthesizes the history of Portugal in a highly nationalistic style, Villagrá reaches back to the foundation story of the Mexica empire the Spanish ruined. This epic strategy cuts against the grain of Spanish ascendancy. That story, abounding with legendary indigenous figures and supernatural occurrences, establishes the epic logic and poetic imagination against which every succeeding canto must be measured. Throughout the poem, but especially in the Acoma cantos so closely modeled after classical epic, Villagrá fashions indigenous characters whose sentiments and dramatic speeches both sentimentalize and demonize "*los indios bárvaros.*" However obviously European, these staged speeches disclose the vast disequilibrium in power relations between native peoples and the Spanish.

As I will argue in the following three chapters, whose divisions I have modeled after the tripartite structure of Villagrá's own narrative, this poet understood the competing subtleties of epic structure and figurative language: he could dedicate his work to the King, who was the State, and yet, through careful rhetorical circumlocution and structural anomaly, critique the empire he celebrated. Historical consciousness colludes here with epic invention. Figurative language masks political chagrin. Perhaps he learned these skills from Virgil, who survived Augustus's wrath by creating an imperial genealogy for his emperor at the same time that he engaged in subtle critique of imperial Rome. Indeed it seems to me that Villagrá knew very well that his epic would stand in immediate comparison to Virgil's *Aeneid*, though with a signal difference: while Aeneas remains the hero-conqueror and progenitor of Rome, Juan de Oñate is saluted as another Aeneas in the opening canto only to be gradually but relentlessly reduced in stature such that his greatest heroic feat dwindles to the fording of the Rio Grande, a river that even in the late sixteenth century hardly compared with the great waterways of Spain. As though to seal this figure of failure, Juan de Oñate, unlike his classical predecessors Odysseus, Achilles, and Aeneas, never leads the charge into battle, nor does he ever fight at the side of his men—rather he is entirely absent from the war against Acoma, having been sent back to the settlement to await the outcome, together with the women and children. Villagrá likewise parodies the Viceroy and the court officials for their indecision, political intrigue, and the bureaucratic red tape that stalled the expedition for nearly three years. In the same stanzaic breath in which he honors the King and beseeches him to remember his loyal soldiers, Villagrá also offers a sharp rebuke for making beggars of the men who have served him in good faith. Indeed, he dedicates an entire canto (20) to delineating the sacrifices soldiers make for King and nation, one example of which we read here:

> Viven y passan casi todo el tiempo
> Como si fueran brutos por el campo,
> Sugetos al rigor del Sol ardiente,
> Al agua, al viento, desnudez y frío,
> Hambre, sed, molimientos y cansancio,
> Cuio lecho no es más que el suelo (20.104–9)

(They live and pass their time out in the fields as though they were brute beasts, subjected to the burning sun, to water, wind, nakedness, and cold, their bed being but hard ground). And, all this in a foreign land, only to return to the palace of the realm, "estropeados, cansados y tullidos" (crippled, worn out and maimed, 20.197), only to be regarded as scum, recognized only by one's dog. Villagrá's explicit allusion to Homer's Ulysses ("Ulixes valeroso") functions as a cunning, and audacious, reminder to the King, his first reader, that empire's soldiers return home to nothing.[6] Those within the palace walls, by contrast, are "muy limpia y olorosa, / Almidonada, rica y bien luzida" (very clean, sweet-smelling / Well-starched, rich, and very pale).[7] Without speaking treason, perhaps Villagrá imagines eviscerating these sweet-smelling, well-starched courtiers he and other soldiers have traveled across the world to enrich. Such is the work of epic, which even in the hands of a minor poet can be made to celebrate and yet skewer empire.

~ 3 ~

Villagrá's *Historia* ends with the poet suggesting he will write another sequence of cantos to fill out the story of la nueva México. Alonso de Ercilla published *La Araucana* in three parts over a period of twenty years, and perhaps that is what Villagrá initially intended for his own project.[8] Some scholars still hope to locate a manuscript sequel in an archive somewhere in Spain, perhaps in Sevilla or Madrid, but I do not think there is anything to be found. If Villagrá did continue to write after learning that Oñate had been ordered to leave the territory and after la nueva México had ground down to a small group of stragglers bent on removing to yet another location, I believe he simply put down his quill one night, gathered whatever he had toiled over, and burned it. What more was there to write about the founding of what was to be a grand Spanish colony in the far north? San Juan de los Caballeros was a failed dream. On April 30, 1610, the same month that Villagrá's *Historia de la Nueva Mexico* was published in Alcalá, Juan de Oñate rode into Mexico City, humiliated, taken down by his own hubris.[9] This was the last conquistador, whose statues today still rouse pride within a small group of culturally ossified "direct descendents," while inciting profound fury in native people who have passed stories from generation to generation telling the truth about him and about one of their villages devastated.

Within two years of its establishment in 1598, only about a third of the settlement's colonists remained in San Juan. In 1601, Oñate relocated what was left of the Spanish settlement across the Rio Grande to a semi-abandoned Tewa village, Yunque-Yunque, and renamed it San Gabriel. What remained of the colony was in shambles, the colonists themselves demoralized, frightened, and disillusioned.[10] Over the course of the next few years, many of those who returned to Mexico banded together to charge Oñate with various acts of tyranny and succeeded in having him deposed. The once-powerful *gobernador* resigned in 1607, about the same time a group of colonists moved some twenty miles south to a small river plateau at the foot of the Sangre de Cristo mountain range to establish Santa Fe. As Oñate, justly humiliated, was riding toward Mexico in 1609, Pedro de Peralta, assigned to be the new governor of la nueva México, arrived in Santa Fe, where he inaugurated a new seat of government in 1610. Ten years later Villagrá died aboard a galleon headed back to the Americas to serve as the newly appointed *alcalde mayor* of Zapotitlán,

Guatemala. This was 1620, the same year the Acoma people were officially allowed to return to their mesa home to begin rebuilding their lives. Like countless mariners before him, he was buried at sea. I imagine his body floating down into the watery depths, hopes dashed one final time. He was sixty-five years old and had spent the decade in Spain politicking for a post somewhere in that faraway world where he was born and of which he had written in the poem that made no mark of success over the ten years. It was as though he spiraled downward into the sea with the poem tucked under his coverlet, the world of print itself a sea that covered over his book as it has so many others. Three hundred years later, his *Historia* washed ashore and was republished in 1900 in Mexico, as a prose story in 1933, and then twice more, in Spain and New Mexico, at the end of the twentieth century.[11] Those of us reading it now will view it differently and will argue over it. Good. There is sufficient fullness and range in its thirty-four cantos to sustain multiple readings. My own reading situates it both in the cultural landscape of its genesis four hundred years ago and today, in a region where the past and present often blur into one another to establish a heroic tradition the poem itself invokes and then largely, I believe, destabilizes.

CHAPTER 1

Fables of la nueva México

Not long ago, I gazed incredulously at the bronze statuary commemorating the Spanish colonial settlement of la nueva México in 1598 that stands outside the Albuquerque Museum. Placed in the museum's sculpture garden in 2005, the life-size metal figures of soldiers, women, and children dominate the landscape. Some are cast on horseback. Others are represented riding in carretas or walking with the livestock. Trudging north, these Spanish settlers had journeyed a thousand miles through rough terrain to insist themselves upon the native people who had inhabited this high-desert world for centuries. Looking at this exhibit, I was stunned, not only because its aesthetic seems so old-fashioned—in this sense it is but one of many of the region's sentimental memorials to the past—but also because its presence must remain a slap in the face of native Americans, especially the Pueblo people, whose dislocation it represents. The sculptural romance of Spanish colonization marks the inception of a four-hundred-year-old exploitation of native people in New Mexico. "Why," I mumbled to myself, "are we still doing this?" The "we" I refer to is the cultural community in which I was raised, a community with deep mestizo roots, despite its fantasy of pure sixteenth-century Spanish origins. Even before I asked some local scholars how this statue came to be placed here, though, I knew that symbolic blood must have been spilled over its installation. Sure enough, as University of New Mexico professor Phillip (Felipe) Gonzales told me later that day, the project had indeed peeled back the bandages of old wounds. Verbal battle took place in the city council, the newspapers, cultural symposia, and town halls. Even the legislature got involved. The installation, Gonzales explained, is actually the result of compromise: the Spanish colonial advocates had initially wanted a large statue of Juan de Oñate, the leader of the expedition, who has over the last century been transformed from the failure he was to a figure of veneration—adelantado, general, and first governor of New Mexico.¹ Ironically, however, the petition for a statue of Oñate had resulted in an installation that represented the entire settlement—complete with a retaining wall listing the names of the 570 people who had made the trek. Unnamed but unmistakable, Oñate stands at the head of the group, heroic in helmet, battle breastplate, and regal cape, one hand on his sword sheath and the other on the King's scroll of contract, looking north toward Ohkay Owingeh, the pueblo just beyond Santa Fe he would christen San Juan de los Caballeros. What you do not read on any of the plaques, of course, is that in 1599 Oñate's soldiers devastated the pueblo of Acoma and that soon after 1600, most of the colonists, feeling this less than glorious leader had duped them, picked up their gear while he was away treasure hunting and returned to Mexico, or to Spain, disillusioned and far poorer than when they had signed on a few years before.

While I am chagrined at this idealization of Spanish New Mexico, I have chosen to read one of the epics of empire that tells the story of this first incursion. Gaspar Pérez de Villagrá's epic *Historia de la Nueva Mexico* is considered one of the earliest narratives to celebrate that late sixteenth-century colonial enterprise. Villagrá writes in a genre that usually celebrates heroic action, recalls a mythos of the nation, dramatizes the battles that install empire, and then projects a people's proud future as part of a great empire. His own epic, it turns out, tells a more complex tale of settlement. This soldier, I am convinced, celebrates not Oñate's heroism but that of the common soldiers and settlers who felt a foolhardy leader had exploited and duped them. Certainly Villagrá recalls the imperial mythos of a nation expanding its geography of power. Yet in the last long movement of the poem, he details the savage, quick destruction of the rebellious Acoma people. His epic projects a future for the Spaniards cursed for the cruelty of their natal colonial encounters with indigenous people.

~ 1 ~

Let me begin at the end of the poem.

In the final scene of Villagrá's *Historia de la Nueva Mexico*, after Acoma has been destroyed, two native warriors ask for knives to cut their own throats as a final defiant offering to the Spaniards, who, apparently not content with having consumed "generosa sangre" (34.281), may perhaps be satisfied at last with their life blood. The two Acoma men would rather kill themselves than allow the Spanish to "stain" them "con manos tan infames y tan viles" (34.290)—with their loathsome and vile hands. Rather than being given knives, however, the men are handed ropes. They walk to a large cottonwood tree with the nooses already tied around their necks and climb to the strongest branches. Just before they hang themselves, Villagrá writes, they curse the Spanish:

> Soldados, advertid que aquí colgados
> Destos rollizos troncos os dexamos
> Los miserables cuerpos por despojos
> De la victoria ilustre que alcanzastes
> De aquellos desdichados que podridos
> Están sobre su sangre rebolcados (34.348–53)

(Soldiers, take heed that hanging here / From these strong branches we bequeath you / Our miserable bodies as spoils / Of the illustrious victory you have won / Against those unfortunate ones, / Who are rotting, mired in their own blood [translation mine].)

Their pueblo home burned to the ground, their loved ones killed or taken prisoner, the two mockingly tell the Spaniards, "y libres nuestras tierras os dexamos" (34.359)—now that our lands are free, we leave them to you. "Dormid a sueño suelto" (34.360)—sleep well, they sneer, and brazenly peering at the crowd they speak a curse that will haunt the Spanish settlement in the years after Acoma's destruction:

> Más de una cosa ciertos os hazemos
> Que si bolver podemos a vengarnos
> Que no parieron madres Castellanas
> Ni bárbaras tampoco, en todo el mundo
> Más desdichados hijos que a vosotros. (34.363–67)

If they can return and witness vengeance, they vow that the children born to Spanish mothers or to their Indian collaborators will be the most unfortunate in all the world. As the two step off the cottonwood branch to their bitter doom, Villagrá's epic of thirty-four cantos in some twelve thousand lines closes, the poem's final haunting image not a celebration of empire but the specter of two corpses swinging in literary space. "Dexándolos colgados, ya me es fuerza / Poner silencio al canto desabrido" (34.384–85)—leaving them hanging, Villagrá writes, I must force myself to silence this harsh canto.

The *Aeneid*, upon which this Spanish poem is modeled, ends when Aeneas plunges his sword into the rebel Turnus's heart, ending for good any Latin conspiracy to undermine imperial Rome. Villagrá might have likewise confirmed Spain's empire, for the penultimate canto ends with Juan de Zaldívar, the Spanish leader of the Acoma expedition, mourning his brother Vicente's death as Aeneas mourns Pallas's, declaiming the final battle and then kneeling in prayer of thanks for victory. Had the poem ended here, the Spanish colonial imagination would have enjoyed an epic song cementing imperial intent at the northernmost frontier of another Rome.[2] Ending as it does, however, with two Acoma warriors derisively conceding their land upon which no gold, silver, pearls, or other fantasy treasure would ever be found, the *Historia* discloses Villagrá's moral dilemma. Of course, by dedicating the epic to Felipe III, he would play to the King and court so as to curry personal favor. He was no fool, after all, and if the empire was in doubt, as was increasingly clear after 1600, he knew he would have to look to his own material needs and future prospects. Yet in the *Historia*, Villagrá also offered a sustained meditation on the lure of wealth la otra México promised, a greed he confesses to sharing. Villagrá seems to be telling himself how foolish the Spanish were for disregarding those *relaciones*, letters, and other official documents he catalogues in his own verse account and that were, every one, clear on the matter: there was no other Tenochtitlán, no Gran Quivira, no El Dorado. While the Spanish had lullabied themselves with stories of Indian chiefs lying under trees listening to chimes made of gold, they discovered in la nueva México merely their own self-deceit, hubris, and cruelty.

Villagrá seems to have known this. In the spring of 1599, just a few months after the assault on Acoma, he rode to Mexico at Oñate's behest to enlist more colonists and supplies for the province. Although he wrote a letter to the Viceroy offering a glowing account of the terrain to generate enthusiasm for the new settlement, Villagrá was not among the recruits who, a full year later, reached San Juan on Christmas Eve of 1600.

~ 2 ~

By 1610 the promise of la nueva México had proven a dismal failure. The new country had not produced a centavo for Spain, much less a kingdom of gold and silver. As the Viceroy in Mexico City wrote to the King on March 31, 1605, "The light that we have thus far gathered on this expedition reveals that the native people are rustic, wretched in clothes and spirit, that they do not possess silver or gold, dwell in straw and grass houses.... [and] instead of cotton, I have been assured that they weave dog hair.... Both the time and expenditure put into this venture," he warned the King, "will be wasted, or at best it is a gamble, as its success rests on flimsy and doubtful information." A few months later, after reading another letter from Oñate dated August 7 that embellished earlier reports of his expedition to the Gulf of California and boasting the "extraordinary riches and monstrosities never heard of before," the Viceroy had had enough. "I cannot but inform your majesty that this conquest is becoming a fairy tale," he reported to the King. "If those who write the reports imagine that they are believed by those who read them, they are greatly mistaken."[3] Less than two years later, Oñate was deposed as governor and ordered to return to Mexico under a cloud of allegations.

Like Francisco Vázquez de Coronado, who some sixty years earlier had led the first large-scale fortune-seeking expedition through la nueva México and ended up riding around in circles for two years, a humiliated Oñate returned to Mexico where he was brought up on thirty charges in 1614. These included "undue severity in punishing the pueblo of Acoma," ordering Villagrá to pursue and execute a group of deserters, and, as the charges registered the many complaints of his own colonists, for living an immoral life with at least one woman, and, finally, that he had "delighted in mocking and insulting ... the royal inspector of his forces."[4]

If we step back a few years to 1600, we begin to understand why Villagrá refused to return to la nueva México. When Oñate sent him to Mexico in the spring of 1599 to recruit new colonists, Villagrá did his duty, persuading some seventy-three colonists to join the expedition. When it came time to return to la nueva México in September 1600, though, using as pretext his inability to serve another officer who was put in charge of the expedition, Villagrá left the company and never again set foot in la nueva México. So much for his loyalty to Oñate and Spain's grand expedition.

Yet strangely, his experience in this remote and severe land provided the imaginative locus for the long poem he published ten years later. Villagrá was probably in Spain by 1605, perhaps already drafting stanzas of the poem that would grow to be thirty-four cantos. Having been educated in law

CHAPTER I

at the Universidad de Salamanca as a young man, he could hardly have returned to Spain from the ends of the earth only to ignore the wealth of learning and culture, the literature and theater enjoying its golden age. Residing in the heart of empire, an ocean away from Oñate's fairy-tale world, he could enjoy these proliferations of culture, purchased, of course, with the wealth of the Americas. Given the wide field of allusion he offers in the *Historia*, he must have been rereading the classical epics, Roman history, and the Aristotelian philosophy he studied as a young Mexican-born criollo whose Spanish parents had sent him to enjoy an education in one of Europe's oldest and greatest universities. The epic vocabulary, character sketching, and oratorical sequences we observe in the last third of his poem are modeled upon Homer and Virgil. The Spanish poet himself notes in his prologue that the foundational Roman history of Titus Livy (59 BC–AD 17) inspired him to preserve the events he witnessed as a warrant against the passage of time and the frailty of memory: "el pueblo Romano en perder lo mucho que de las historias de Ticolivio su coronista nos infalta, que el la declinación y ruyna de su Imperio, y monarchia que fue la mayor del mundo" (the Roman people were more endangered by the loss of Titus Livy's histories than of the decline and fall of the Empire and the monarchy, which was the greatest in the world).⁵ Coupled with the Greek and Roman texts that inform the imaginative structure of the *Historia*, Villagrá's comments about the irreparable loss of Livy's writings suggest that written narrative rather than empire itself provides a people with their legacy.

However indebted to Greco-Roman writers—we know he read Lucan, the Roman Spaniard who around AD 63 wrote the *Pharsalia* chronicling the battles between Caesar and Pompey in 49 BC—Villagrá was equally familiar with the proliferating New World epics: Saavedra Guzmán's *El peregrino indiano*, Laso de la Vega's *Mexicana*, and especially Alonso de Ercillas's *La Araucana*, an account of the resistance of the Araucanian people in Chile in the mid-sixteenth century that is one of the principal models for the Spanish poet's representation of indigenous resistance in the *Historia*. This milieu seemed encouraging for soldiers whose new world adventures could be turned to silver by the pen.

The most famous of his contemporaries, of course, was Miguel de Cervantes. Like Villagrá, he had been just another of the King's veterans

46

before the appearance in 1605 of part one of the magisterial *Don Quixote de la Mancha*. In 1571 Cervantes lost the use of his left arm while fighting in the Battle of Lepanto. Returning to Spain, his ship was captured and he was imprisoned in Algiers for five years. After his release and return to Spain, he was for twenty-five years a struggling writer, supporting his family through what must have been repulsive employment as a grain commissary—a kind of tax collector. Twice during this period, he was thrown in jail for debt. We know little about Villagrá's movements in Spain at this time, but the world of soldier-poets was small, and it is possible that the two writers met. Perhaps they talked of soldiering, of war, of the presence of Spain in the world. Indeed, Cervantes twice petitioned for an official position in the Americas, but in 1590, as earlier in 1582, he was turned down by the bureaucrats both he and Villagrá later vilified in their writing.[6]

Upon his return to Spain, Villagrá must have been caught up in the Cervantine energy of the time. I imagine him laughing through long passages of *Don Quixote*, which was in its first moment not a classic but the thrill of the town and a best seller that showed how a man of arms might profit by turning from sword to pen. Given his allusion to Numantia in the *Historia*, Villagrá likely read or saw a performance of the novelist's *El cerco de Numancia* (staged first circa 1583–85), a four-act play that dramatizes the Celtiberian resistance to the Romans that in 133 BC culminated in a battle whose outcome—the decision of the Numantians to commit mass suicide rather than surrender—bore an uncanny resemblance to his representation of Acoma's resistance in 1599.

As a young man, Villagrá had spent the 1580s currying position in Felipe II's court. After his return to Madrid, he must have walked through the lively streets looking up and down the rows of houses, taverns, and shops, all the while remembering the nights on a trail at the end of the world, the desert heat cooling in the evening, the great river he and the other soldiers had followed, the grassy plains where they beheld vast herds of bison and hunted side by side with scores of native people. He had left the expedition in 1599, angry and disillusioned, like many of the other soldiers who had endured much privation and then returned to Spain to be treated like beggars. Musing in the capital a quarter century later, he must have recalled with chagrin the chimera of wealth he and the others had pursued across wide stretches of open country. Then, like a soldier, he would have regained his bearings and gone on through the street to a *taberna* to join those eating tortas and drinking *tinto*.

CHAPTER I

The frontispiece etching from the 1610 edition of the *Historia* provides Villagrá's sole likeness. Here he is balding but has a heavy mustache, his brow etched with heavy furrows, a muscular man and somewhat short, as noted in the one of the expedition documents. It is this well-muscled, serious man with lined brow I imagine sitting in the audience at one of the myriad Lope de Vega plays performed throughout Spain. Perhaps after the theater he sat at his table late into the night reading those scenes in *Don Quixote* by which Cervantes dismantles books of chivalry for their aesthetic irregularities, unbelievable actions, lovesick girls fawning over heroic knights, strange dwarves and fantastic monsters, nonsensical journeys, and foolish language.[7] Indeed, some of the literary figures Cervantes parodied in *Quixote* found their way into Villagrá's own verse recollection of a journey that was at once true and fantastic in its blurring of chronicle and epic poetry.

As a man who had seen death up close and had come to understand battle in ways the student he had been years earlier in Salamanca could not, Villagrá would have returned to the classical writers, rereading the meandering journeys and battle scenes Virgil described in the *Aeneid*. He must have remembered his own audacious, epic journey, riding a thousand miles on horseback and encountering the indigenous people and cultures Cabeza de Vaca had described seventy years before Oñate's expedition. He would have recalled his first sighting of Acoma, the citadel on a sandstone mesa that a precursor had called "the most secure fortress in all the world."[8] He could not have forgotten how wooden spikes tore his horse apart by or how he had fallen headlong into one of the pit traps the Acoma had set for their defense, nor had he forgotten how he clawed and crawled his way out, walking for days through the snow, fearful and disoriented, or how he had stabbed his own loyal dog for food, calling to it after it fled in confusion, and cradling the dying animal while it licked its own blood from his hands. Writing this episode and himself as a character in his story, Villagrá marks a moment of profound self-doubt, fear, and unsoldierly desperation. He further narratively opens to the recreation of an even darker recollection: thirteen of his Spanish comrades, heedless and arrogant, are killed atop Acoma after stealing supplies, corn, and a woman's turkey. A month later, seventy soldiers in full battle armor with vengeance in their hearts rode to Acoma, destroyed the village, and slaughtered hundreds of people whose blood bathed the walls of the mesa fortress they believed was invincible.

Reading these final cantos of Acoma's destruction discloses a moral corruption the bluster of epic battle scenes cannot suppress. Villagrá writes too much, describes what he ought not, and in so doing exposes Spanish viciousness, but the truth must out. Villagrá winced in retrospect at how easy killing had been, there, so far away, in that other world. Then as now, I believe, soldiers did not kill without nightmare confusion afterward. So it seems to me that Acoma, the desert, Cervantes's *Numancia*, the *Aeneid*, Ercilla's *Araucana*, much of the Trojan cycle, and stories of the Conquest of Mexico told a century earlier would have crowded upon Villagrá. Not unlike Cervantes, who proudly remembered his part in the battle against the Turks and in *Numancia* simultaneously celebrated ancient Spain's valor against Rome and questioned the sixteenth-century Spaniards who behaved like Romans, Villagrá, I am convinced, would have been proud of Spain's empire yet perturbed at recalling its slaughter of a proud and largely peaceful people.

All this must have concentrated itself within him until audacious, suddenly late one night or some afternoon, he set pen to paper. Villagrá would have recalled not the chivalric narrative of *Amadis of Gaul* and its puerile clan but the heroes of classical epic. He was a soldier, after all, not a "sweet-smelling" courtier who turned the pages of romances with dainty fingers. When he began to write, he would remember war. "Las armas y el varón heroico canto" (1.1) he wrote to open his own poem, echoing the first stanza of the *Aeneid*'s opening lines ("Arma virumque cano . . ."—I sing of arms and the man who first from Troy's shores[9]), which in turn recalled the cadence of Homer's *Odyssey*—"Sing to me of the man, Muse, the man of twists and turns / driven time and again off course, once he had plundered the hallowed heights of Troy."[10] Then, *poco a poco*, he remembers and imagines, compares one epic with another, daringly chanting his words alongside theirs. In remembering his own Troy at Acoma, he likens the Spanish empire to the civilization that, centuries earlier, had assimilated his own people within its huge expanse. As he quills notes to himself, he writes phrase upon phrase, tens, and then hundreds of lines of verse, until in the final battle cantos, ink spills across the pages like black blood.

New Spain—las Américas—was still being discovered, explored, and mapped at its furthest reaches. Always just beyond the *plus ultra* of the known terrain, a fantasy still enticed the Spanish imagination, one or another story of glimmering cities wreathed in gold. Another Tenochtitlán to be despoiled. By the time he had returned to Spain and while drafting lines, Villagrá knew these for fairy tales. Perhaps, though, he might sell a soldier's tale of exploration, a story of encounters with "los indios bárbaros" in an ocean of grassland where huge beasts—*vacas*—or buffalo, as we know them, dominated the horizon for hundreds of leagues in every direction. Because epic requires war, there would of course be a battle against a fiercely independent, courageous people living atop a stone fortress that would remind Spaniards of Numantia. Villagrá, the well-educated but foolish soldier who had set out two decades earlier for una otra México, for gold and silver, had returned to the King's circle empty-handed. Yet a story in verse might appeal to a Spanish audience fascinated with the Americas, and if dedicated to the King, such heroic poetry might renew his favor, whether the book sold or not. Who better to tell such a tale than one of the King's soldiers, a witness to the events of the first settlement, who could tell the story of la nueva México even as he carefully dissociated himself from its failure by dimming Oñate's presence in the story.

Villagrá would have encountered the usual worries about how best to narrate the story of Spain's venture and his own. Perhaps he should write a first-person history of the settlement of la nueva México, personal narrative and official history linked into a narrative structure that would stand as a soldier's account of life in a fabulous, distant unknown. There were, after all, precedents for such chronicles of exploration and conquest. Bernal Díaz del Castillo wrote one of the first accounts of the Conquest of Mexico from a common soldier's point of view;[11] Álvar Núñez Cabeza de Vaca's *Relación* (1536)[12] charted the vast territory between Florida and what is now the Southwest; Pedro de Castañeda de Nájera penned a narrative of the first major Spanish expedition into la nueva México in 1540.[13] Villagrá read many such relaciones by soldiers and alludes to them in the *Historia*, a poem that to this day historians less interested in Villagrá the poet than in Villagrá the soldier-chronicler rely on.

Perhaps Villagrá's focus upon the expedition explains why his critics, then and today, argue he should have stuck to history. Court censor Vicente Espinel noted in the book's prefatory pages that the "verses are many and though lacking invention and poetical worth are a true and connected history." Three hundred years later, Luis González Obregón states in the 1900 edition that Villagrá "was a poet-chronicler, but more of a chronicler than a poet." Herbert Bolton, the early twentieth-century Spanish borderlands historian, suggests that the "work, while written in verse, is in reality an important source based upon the author's personal experience and documentary data."[14] These assessments seem to me wrong from beginning to end, for Villagrá at every turn makes history subordinate to an idea of history as literary subject. His is a narrative poem in which chronicle is subject to the permutations of the imagination as well as to those structures of this genre: the hendecasyllabic line, the rich field of metaphor and allusion drawn from myriad literary sources, invocations, mythic fables and characters, and dramatic oratory modeled from classical and New World sources. One can certainly argue that Villagrá was a minor poet, one unprepared for the onerous requirements the form he chose imposes, but to insist that his work merely fulfills the function of chronicle, that it is a "true history" of the Oñate expedition based upon "documentary data," is unimaginative. Worse, it makes me wonder what we have for "history" when historians read the poem as a text to be trusted for the truth rather than as epic, a genre that has greater loyalty to the imagination and to a long literary tradition of mythic history than to chronicle.

Perhaps the most egregious misunderstanding of Villagra's knowing manipulation of poetry and history comes from Marc Simmons, one of the preeminent historians of Spanish colonial New Mexico, who in his 1991 study *The Last Conquistador* writes that while Villagrá was "an eyewitness to many of the events he describes, his verses are weighted with rhetorical flourishes, moral platitudes, and references to classical authors."[15] I must agree: unfortunately for historians, Villagrá's *Historia de la Nueva Mexico* is an epic replete with the "rhetorical flourishes" that are the common material of poetry. The ethical principles common to Renaissance poets may be moral platitudes to us, but these clichés nonetheless provided them with a spiritual compass in a world structured by religious and military institutions. The "references to classical authors" place Villagrá's work within a literary matrix that makes clear his intention to render "eyewitness" history in symbolic language, language permeated by classical allusion, epic oratory that poses moral questions about empire, scenes of devastation drawn from the ancients that speak to the brutality of war across the centuries.

Once he chose the genre, the structure of epic decided the order and magnitude of the story. With this decision Villagrá effectively made history subordinate to verse. Whoever reads his poem de la nueva México will indeed find the discourses of the official archive interpolated into the poem: long letters, itinerary reports, earlier relaciones, and cedulas, legal documents that carried the king's orders to his subjects across an ocean and two continents. This idea of history has to be understood, however, through the intertextual imbrications of earlier epic woven into the Spanish poet's narrative. Acoma stands as Troy not so much to occlude what took place on the mesa, but, I believe, because the *Iliad* and the *Aeneid* bring clarity to the brutality and rage that took place in la nueva México. Like Ercilla, the soldier-poet who did his share of killing native people in Chile, Villagrá found a way to confront his own murderous rage in the imaginative structure of verse, poetry making lucid and stark the violence he had committed. In that relation between poetry as a meditation on personal culpability and culpability locked to the social structures that determine personal action, the *Historia* often turns upon the rhetorics of ethical behavior twinned to sixteenth-century Roman Catholic doctrine and the imperial ideology that buttressed the Spanish conquest. This stands over and against Villagrá's personal disclosures on the corrosive effects of greed for gold, his bitterness at feeling abandoned by King and Church after enduring deprivation of all sorts, his fear of death in a remote land, and, finally, his recognition of the role he played in the murder of Pueblo people.

The *Historia* is not strictly a confessional, but it does disclose transgression. In 1614, Oñate was convicted of twelve of the thirty charges fellow colonists, various officials, and the Viceroy leveled against him. One of the charges, in official legal discourse, as George Hammond documents, is that "said don Juan de Oñate caused two Indians of the town of Acoma to be hanged," allegedly for killing a Mexican Indian, one of the hundreds who had been brought along on the expedition.[16] Villagrá would have known about this execution by hanging, but he reframes the official act as epic commentary, allegorizing rather than chronicling history. Here, Villagrá turns the historical incident and its record into a startling narrative voicing of indigenous recrimination, resentment, and hatred—all gathering into a knot of language that curses the Spaniards for their brutality. The massacre at Acoma is one of the scenes the soldier-poet cannot tear from memory, refusing to cover it up or reduce it to summary document. He chooses instead to evoke it as the seal that concludes the poem, a blood seal that once and for all exposes Spanish cruelty. In this way, epic admits what the official report denies.

The malediction with which Villagrá concludes his poem, as scholars such as David Quint have pointed out, is standard fare in epics of power and empire, having the staged effect, they argue, of sentimentalizing and recontaining resistance.[17] Villagrá's version of these last words in the poem is indeed more epic than historically accurate—the Spaniards hanged two Acoma men at Oñate's order. If you are reading for a version of the cruelty and destruction the Spanish left in the wake of their greed for gold, however, the epic speech will linger in a way the official record does not, in no small measure because the official record we have is sparse, a paragraph here or a note there without commentary. More often, the something that happened was suppressed or simply expunged. That a Spaniard such as Villagrá would give voice to Indian contempt and hatred implicates him as one of the King's soldiers ordered to execute the empire's retribution against this and future uprisings. As eyewitness, Villagrá reconstructs the battle at Acoma as a theater of unequal violence, pouring his own spiritual nausea back into the poem to remind his readers, even today, that the history of Spanish presence in la nueva México is one of disruption and despoliation. How else understand the final words of the two Acoma warriors? "Soldiers, take heed that hanging here ... we bequeath you / Our miserable bodies as spoils / Of the illustrious victory you have won" (34.345–48 [translation mine]).

For their isolated uprising in December 1599, these mesa people were massacred by the hundreds, their mangled bodies left in tangled heaps, their blood congealing on their high-desert home. Illustrious? No, the battle lasted but two days, and only one Spanish soldier was killed, accidentally by another Spaniard. The survivors were marched a hundred miles to what became Santo Domingo Pueblo, where they were shamed at a mock trial, women and children sentenced to servitude for twenty years. Oñate then ordered all men older than twenty-five to undergo amputation; each had a foot chopped off. The elders were sent off to different pueblos, while the girls were dispatched to convents in Mexico. This humiliation becomes a four-hundred-year-old grudge that refuses to blithely vanish despite the Land of Enchantment tourist discourse that celebrates New Mexico's tricultural heritage. On the contrary: when you visit Acoma Pueblo today, you will be told, briefly but with unbridled clarity, what the Spaniards did in 1599. Yet the inhabitants of Sky City, as Acoma advertises itself for the benefit of thousands of tourists who visit each year from all over the world, generally do not dwell upon the massacre, preferring to note that Acoma is the oldest, continuously inhabited city in the United States. Paradoxically, it is Villagrá's epic poem that remembers the walls of that sky city washed in its own blood.

CHAPTER I

~ 3 ~

Now we can start at the beginning of the poem. *Historia de la Nueva Mexico* opens unmistakably with Virgil's cadence and phrasing, invoking the heroic figure of Aeneas as the model for Juan de Oñate, the leader of the Spanish expedition.

> Las armas y el varón heroico canto,
> El ser, valor, prudencia y alto esfuerzo
> De aquel cuya paciencia no rendida,
> Por un mar de disgustos arrojada,
> A pesar de la envidia ponzoñosa
> Los hechos y prohezas va encumbrando
> De aquellos españoles valerosos
> Que en la Occidental India remontados,
> Descubriendo del mundo lo que esconde,
> "Plus ultra" con braveza van diziendo
> A fuerza de valor y brazos fuertes,
> En armas y quebrantos tan sufridos
> Quanto de tosca pluma celebrados. (1.1–13)

(I sing of arms and the heroic man, / The being, courage, care, and high emprise / Of him whose unconquered patience, / Though cast upon a sea of cares, / In spite of envy slanderous, / Is raising to new heights the feats, / The deeds, of those brave Spaniards who, / In the far India of the West, / Discovering in the world that which was hid, / "Plus ultra" go bravely saying / By force of valor and strong arms, / In war and suffering as experienced / As celebrated now by pen unskilled.)

As in Virgil's epic invocation, Homer also spirals into the *Historia* at its outset. At first glance, it appears we will read an epinician ode to the Spanish conquest. In Homer and Virgil, we are at once located in the midst of crisis over which our hero will prevail, and, although the hero may not be named outright, readers soon understand that Odysseus and Aeneas are the men of arms and valor whose force, wit, and courage bring crisis to resolution, even if it takes years of circuitous journeying and the surmounting of numerous obstacles. Those contemporary readers of Villagrá familiar with Virgil's epic of the mythic foundations of the Roman Empire would look for a Spanish Aeneas in Villagrá's tale about the establishment of la nueva México. Juan de Oñate is, or should be, that figure. If at first glance Oñate is the "varón heroico" who leads an expedition a thousand miles across the parched desert of northern Mexico to settle a frontier, Villagrá soon troubles facile connection between the Roman hero and this Spanish general as the first stanza shifts decisively from its focus on a single hero—Oñate—to "aquellos españoles valerosos," those valiant soldiers who, by "force of valor and strong arms," have expanded the empire's reach into the "plus ultra," that hidden terrain that lies beyond the map. From the start, it is their heroism Villagrá sings.

In a richly suggestive, if brief, essay published in *The Bilingual Review*, Philadelphio Jaramillo summarizes this dissonance. "It is clear from the first canto that Villagrá's epic hero was meant to be don Juan de Oñate.... The real hero of the poem, however, is not [Oñate], but a collective protagonist, as in Ercilla's *La Araucana*; in this case, the Spanish soldier-settlers.... The feats of the individual soldiers are sung throughout the poem, to the extent that the soldiers take on a more important role than that played by their leader."[18] These are the *valerosos* who have furthered the reaches of empire by traveling beyond the point of no return; men who have proven their valor, suffered deprivation, fought the King's battles, and, later in the poem, are scorned as little more than beggars when they seek remuneration for their services to the crown. Whereas Aeneas, "Fate's fugitive," has been tossed about on land and sea by the gods, Oñate has been subject not to the opposition of Juno but merely the "envidia ponzoñosa" (slanderous envy) of royal bureaucrats who have delayed his expedition with their conniving plots ("un mar de disgustos arrojada") to wrestle away the settlement contract. Villagrá dedicates his poem to the King because he must, but it is for his friends, the common soldiers, that he writes:

> Sólo resta que aquellos valerosos
> Por quien este cuydado yo he tomado
> Alienten con su gran valor heroico
> El atrevido buelo de mi pluma
> Porque desta vez pienso que veremos
> Yguales las palabras con las obras. (1.41–46)

('Tis only required that those same brave men / For whom this task I undertook / Should nourish with their great, heroic valor / The daring flight of this my pen, / Because I think that this time we shall see / The words well equaled by the deeds.)

This tribute creates a major problem for the poem. Valorous soldiers commonly play minor parts in epic, for the genre typically singles out an Odysseus, an Achilles, an Aeneas as archetypal hero. Villagrá confounds this expectation, not because, as he pretends, his pen is unskilled ("tosca pluma," 1.13), but because history has given him no rationale to raise Oñate to such stature: by 1610, this general's expedition to la nueva México was widely considered a failure. Given Oñate's diminishing stature in the eyes of the court and his eventual incrimination, Villagrá, who wished to win the King's approval, is not likely to have glorified this explorer as the hero of a poem about Spanish adventure in the New World. In fact, the *Historia* is dedicated to Felipe III, whom Villagrá praises as the "phoenix of new Mexico" (1.15) and about whom, through his poem, "The whole world shall listen" (1.34). Such praise is shameless self-promotion. Villagrá commemorates the King's mandate: "los hechos / Dignos de que la pluma los levante" (1.37–38) (deeds worthy of being elevated by the pen). His commemoration ultimately chafes at empire, though, when Villagrá alludes to the mistreatment his companions are subjected to when they seek redress from the court for the perils they endured on his behalf. If his monarch shoulders the world, how dare a common soldier like Villagrá undermine his authority? This early expression of doubt in empire will expand as the poem develops and Villagrá as much as commands Felipe III to hear from a soldier: "Listen to me, great King, for I am witness / of all that here, my Lord, I say to you" (1.47–48).

Yet, it is the King's proxy, Juan de Oñate, whom the *Historia* diminishes. He is honorable enough, Jaramillo argues, "the noble son, descendant of a distinguished family, especially qualified to lead this voyage."[19] Jaramillo concedes that Villagrá "resorts to the frequent use of epithets to affirm the heroic image of don Juan, often comparing him to the classical heroes of the past: Achilles, Aeneas, Julius Caesar, and others."[20] Such rhetorical strategies are, I would argue, seldom borne out by heroic action. Oñate's single act of bravado in the poem is to lead the colonists across the Rio Grande as they make their final approach to the new colony, but he is no Moses. Rather in this poem the hero proves to be only flesh and blood, a historic person, patient but confused, who rides hundreds of miles in one direction and then another in a vain attempt to strike it rich, only to fail repeatedly. As Villagrá chronicles these misdirections and lapses in judgment, the poem moves altogether beyond Oñate, who in the final cantos simply disappears in a way unimaginable for the titular hero of Virgil's *Aeneid*.

The great irony in reading and, yes, reclaiming Villagrá's *Historia de la Nueva Mexico* is that, opening as it does, the poem dismantles a heroic colonial fantasy some of Oñate's cultural descendants are working hard to recreate hundreds of years later. The man who lost the trust of most of his colonists within the first year, who ordered the massacre of Acoma, and who failed to find the wealth he was sent for has become the icon for a reinvented Spanish colonial past. Mounted atop a bronze stead, gallant and commanding, an Aeneas of the Southwest, Oñate's statue in Alcalde surveys northern New Mexico just a few miles from the Tewa village he unsettled in 1598—a village that after four hundred years has audaciously and proudly taken down the sign "San Juan Pueblo" and reclaimed its tribal name, Ohkay Owingeh. Standing beneath the metal figure, one cannot help but look for a seam above his boot, which some years back was sawed off in symbolic retribution for his order against the Acoma men.

As condemnatory of our contemporary mythmaking of the Spanish entrada into New Mexico is Villagrá's tribute to a Mesoamerican migration myth developed in the first two cantos. What one ends up remembering about the opening stanzas is not the glorious Spanish journey to settle a new empire, but a story about the origins of the Aztecs and the founding of Tenochtitlán. By comparison, Villagrá presents the stanzas on sixteenth-century exploration that follow as fables of failure that should have warned off the fool's mission he dramatizes. Virgil places Aeneas at the center of a national genealogy that traces Roman lineage directly to ancient Troy. Likewise, Luís Vaz de Camões, Villagrá's Portuguese contemporary, recalls the proud history of the nation in his 1572 epic *Os Lusiadas*, the story of Vasco de Gama's naval conquest of India. Villagrá offers no myth of Iberia, however, nor does he rehearse a heroic story of Spain's rise to world domination; rather he summons the epic migration of the early Aztecas into the lake region where they settled and grew to become one of the great indigenous civilizations in the Americas.

> Destas nuevas Regiones es notario,
> Pública voz y fama que deciden
> Aquellos más antiguos Mexicanos
> Que a la Ciudad de México famosa
> El nombre le pussieron porque fuesse
> Eterna su memoria perdurable (1.85–90)

(It is well known and told by all that from these regions [where we are going] the ancient Mexicans descended and founded the famous city of Mexico, giving it their name as an eternal memorial.)

CHAPTER I

No sooner has the obligatory dedication to the King been put to rest than Villagrá turns our attention to the location of la nueva México under the heavens—"Beneath the Arctic pole, in height / Some thirty-three degrees" (1.49–50)—and then to the story of those "más antiguos Mexicanos," those Mexica people, remembered today as Aztecs, who journeyed from that northern region where the Spanish are headed to found "la Ciudad de México," or Tenochtitlán. All at once we see a fabulous tapestry of native people gathered in the immense desert. Villagrá relates this migration tale as though he has heard native storytellers tell it during the long days and months the Spanish colony waited in Santa Bárbara to begin their long journey. There are hints here of Boccaccio's *Decameron*, of Chaucer's *Canterbury Tales*, and of *The Arabian Nights*—stories told to pass the time as people travel en masse. Seeing that the Spaniards are journeying north, Villagrá writes, the Indians in the region recount an old story of migration from "la tierra adentro" (1.120). In the far north, people emerged from a "hollow, craggy cave" ("cóncava caverna desabrida," 1.121), developed a sophisticated culture and social structure, and then at the behest of two courageous brothers, begin their own migration south to discover a new world. By transcribing this native origin story, Villagrá fashions indigenous epic so that it serves as corollary to the Spanish journey, reminding his readers that origin myths are similar across cultures. Of course, the Spanish poet describes the indigenous throng in language more reminiscent of a sixteenth-century court masque than an Aztec migration. As the scene unfolds, the wandering Aztecs appear like Spanish aristocrats, traveling with "Gran suma de bagage y aparato, / Tiendas y pabellones bien luzidos" (1.146–47) (Piles of baggage and equipment / tents and brightly lit pavilions). We read of an "Infinidad de niños y muchachos / . . . retozando, / Embueltos en juguetes muy donosos" (1.150–52) (An infinity of children / . . . playing / surrounded by beautiful toys). Finally, "There showed themselves among the deadly arms, / As flowers beautiful are seen 'mid thorns, / Fair dames and ladies and bright damsels, / As dainty, lovely, and discreet / . . . And in the very flower of youth, young men, / And gentlemen and well dressed, all, / Each one competing with the rest / Such sum of finery and of livery / As in the finest and most lofty courts / Are accustomed to be worn on the most festal days / By the most conspicuous courtiers") (1.156–67).

Villagrá figures the indigenous camp in distinctly European imagery, one grants, for a Spanish audience that might want to see themselves and their court rituals in a tale of "los bárbaros." Perhaps girls unwittingly smiled at Villagrá's conceit of them as "bellas flores" amid "espinas" (thorns) (1.157), while courtiers puffed up seeing "the very flower of their youth" (1.161) as they matched their strength in play against rivals. Parents, of course, must have imagined their own cherubic children playing "surrounded by beautiful toys." To most of his contemporary readers, Villagrá's scene would have recalled court paintings rather than the inscrutable hieroglyphics they might have caught glimpses of in the Nahautl scrolls then circulating in Europe's royal cliques.

Still, why would an epic of empire open with this idealized recovery of an indigenous origin myth? Especially if, as some scholars have argued, Villagrá's story is intended to justify the assault on the Acoma or preempt the charges of cruelty against native people being marshaled against Oñate's officers as the *Historia* was going to press. I can only say that the poet's representations of intercultural contact are rife with contradiction. Make no mistake: Villagrá is a Spaniard. The native people he and the Oñate party meet are regarded as "bárbaros," a word with a long history of European ethnocentrism about native difference: of language and writing, dress and cultural practice, religious beliefs, and icons and ritual. Of course, religious conversion was the usual excuse given for displacing, brutalizing, and murdering native people. Villagrá the soldier never denies that he participated in military campaigns against native people. Yet a decade after his entrada into la nueva México, Villagrá the poet discloses a more complex understanding of native life and culture than he is usually credited.

The writer opens by recounting an indigenous origin myth he may have heard firsthand, an origin story that he makes equal to the founding of Rome and in so doing, displaces King and empire, not to mention the Viceroy, Oñate, the Zaldívars, and perhaps himself. Had he opened with frightening images of native people, savage in dress and manner, spiritually benighted, led by fanatic *tlatlamine* priests who coerced obedience to a vision of empire in which, the Spanish charged, human hearts were cut out by the thousands to satisfy their god Huitzilopochtli, Villagrá might more effectively have prepared his readers for the massacre at Acoma. If he had written simply to preempt the charges of violence against him as a participant, would he not have wished to figure them as brutish, so that killing hundreds of such savages would pose no moral quandary?

Ercilla represents the Araucanian people sympathetically—but not before describing their culture as one that thrives on warfare, masculine force, contests of strength, body piercing, and ritual cannibalism. Villagrá's "antiguos mexicanos" are radically civilized by comparison, a people who have developed a complex writing system: "aquella antiguísima pintura / y modo hierogliphico que tienen, / Por el qual tratan, hablan y se entienden" (1.94–95) (that very ancient art and hieroglyphic method they have whereby they trade, communicate and are understood).[21] Such representation suggests that while his epic will represent historical events, his deeper interest is both in imagining la nueva México as a land with ancient human communities and in creating an imaginary region where the Spaniards are figured as retracing old migration routes rather than moving through new terrain. Villagrá writes with a sense of wonder about a world foreign to the courtiers who might read his epic but less strange to a man like himself born to this new world.

Of course, as many cantos disclose, Villagrá often retreats from fascination to outrage, largely feigned, I believe, so as to mouth the theological conventions the Church censors expected. Remember that he had to satisfy all the fray de los Reyeses who would scrutinize his poem for any lapses in orthodoxy, conferring the seal that allowed script to go to print: "no é hallado en ella cosa contra la Fé." Villagrá, one can argue, writes from inside the ideology of Spanish Roman Catholicism and believes what he scribes, but over and over what he writes suggests a shift in sensibility in his views of indigenous people. Perhaps he Europeanizes the Aztecas in order to domesticate them, but his representation contravenes the earlier accounts of the friars, who had pictured native people as idolatrous, bound to Satan in their devotion to deities like Huitzilopochtli, Tezcatlipoca, and Coatlicue. Their stone images indeed appeared ferocious but no more so than the European pantheon of hideously martyred saints pierced with arrows and knives, eviscerated, hung upside down, and burned at the stake. Indeed, Spain was saturated with wooden figures of Christ hanging from a cross, blood soaked, in frightful anguish. This thorn-crowned Christ would displace Huitzilopochtli.

Let us return to Villagrá's syncretic story of the ancient Aztec migration. The festive and bright caravan is all at once thrown into fear by the appearance of "aquel maldito" (2.10)—a strange indigenous figure who suddenly appears in the road and, in powerful and direct speech, pirates their journey. This sensational representation would mollify the watchful Church censors as it aroused his audience. The demonic *maldito* was meant to frighten Christian readers, but such figures were common in the ancient world as well as in the European tales Villagrá's contemporaries knew. In the *Historia*, the maldito transforms himself into an old woman, the well-known hag of patriarchal European imagination:

> Truxo el cabello cano mal compuesto
> Y, qual horrenda y fiera notomía
> El rostro descarnado, macilento,
> De fiera y espantosa catadura;
> Desmesurados pechos, largas tetas,
> Hambrientas, flacas, secas y fruncidas,
> Nerbudos pechos, anchos y espaciosos,
> Con terribles espaldas bien trabadas;
> Sumidos ojos de color de fuego,
> Disforme boca desde oreja a oreja,
> Por cuyos labios secos, desmedidos,
> Quatro sólos colmillos hazia fuera
> De un largo palmo, (2.14–44)

(He had his gray hair horridly dressed / And like a hideous, fierce skeleton / His fleshless and emaciated face / Of an expression wild and fearsome, / Misshapen breasts and dangling teats / Starved, flaccid, dry, and wrinkled / ... A mouth malformed, from ear to ear / Through whose dry and distorted lips / Of fangs just four protruded / And, curving, showed themselves a good palm's length.)

While Villagrá's fearsome hermaphroditic figure draws upon European images of devils and gruesome allegorizations of Death, it also leans upon the emerging Renaissance fascination with classical mythology. The editors of the 1992 edition note that his maldito echoes Lucan's Erictho and Homer's Circe, the other more common image of the witch-seer.[22] Similarly, in the Aztec origin story, the powerful deity Huitzilopochtli issues the edict to journey to a location where the tribe shall settle. Before Villagrá wrote the *Historia*, this myth had been preserved in the hieroglyphic codices Bernardino de Sahagún described in his *Historia general de México*. It is possible that Villagrá had looked over Sahagún's work, or perhaps he had perused Juan de Tovar's *Historia de la benida de los indios a poblar de México de las partes remotas de occidente* (History of the Arrival of the Indians who Populated Remote Parts of Western Mexico, c. 1580). After all, he was born in Puebla at a time when native religion, culture, and language were being preserved and studied in order to convert the Indians. The 1992 editors note Villagrá's "anthropological knowledge" and the access he would have had to Sahagún's book, in which he would have seen Aztec-Mexica figures from the codices.[23] There is nothing European about the figures in Sahagún, nor does Sahagún include commentary on the Aztec migration to the Valley of Mexico. Villagrá might have consulted fray Diego de Durán's (1537–88) *Historia de las Indias de Nueva España*, however; there appear to be correspondences between Villagrá's description of the pottery shards and ruins the ancient expedition presumably left along the journey as well as images of Aztec warriors: "armas fuertes, belicosas," "ligeras picas y pesadas mazas," "gruessos bastones con pesados cantos / En sus fuertes bejucos enagastados" (strong and warlike arms, light javelins and heavy maces, thick clubs with heavy stones / embedded in their strong wood) and dressed in the likeness of the "fiera tigre," "suelto pardo," "el hambriento lobo carnicero" (fierce tiger, leopard, hungry, meat-eating wolf) (1.175–200). Such animal costuming of warriors appears in the stunning pictorial manuscripts of the pre-Columbian world, and there is no reason a man born and raised in Puebla in the mid-sixteenth century might not have seen the codices or studied the elegant carvings on temple balustrades, the myriad statues of the deities, the pottery figurines of gods and common people in daily activities, or heard tales of the origin myths and migration stories.

There is little evidence in the *Historia*, however, to suggest that Villagrá consulted Sahagún's *Primeros memoriales*, a collection of Aztec cultural archives that provided the setting for the *Historia general*. Otherwise, Villagrá would likely have included Huitzilopochtli, imaged in all of the codices as a hummingbird with serpent tail or a human face with a hummingbird helmet. Commonly reviled by Spanish clergy as evidence of an idolatry that must be destroyed, this deity is the pivotal figure around which the Aztec migration myth revolved.[24] Perhaps to placate the friars, Villagrá initially presents the maldito as the emissary of the devil, "aqueste gran señor que acá me embía" (that great lord who sent me here, 2.75), but the ancient Mexicans to whom he, like Erictho, delivers the prophesy are never represented as malditos themselves, even though many are dressed in ceremonial animal skins, "the fox, the hare and the rabbit shy / The fishes huge and lordly eagles, too" (1.177–78). Villagrá unites Spain and ancient Mexico in a curious but appealing fusion: the children are innocents, the women are *doncellas*, or beautiful maidens, and all are respectfully referred to as "Aquellos brabos viejos que salieron / De la gran nueva México famosa" (those courageous ancient ones who emerged / from that great and famous new México) (2.278–80).

In Villagrá's Euro-Indo syncretic story, the prophetic figure tells the two brothers who are leading the migration that one of them must return north to "la dulze patria" (2.155) to care for their aged father, while the other is to "pursue his noble star" (2.89). Alluding to earlier epic figures, Villagrá indicates that they will find their "próspero destino" not in Troy, where the ancient Romans saw "the head of Priam struck from off his shoulders," nor to where "the great hide of the beautiful bull / Took up so much land that it was enough / To close within its mighty strips / The lofty walls of Carthage" (2.90–96), but where

> en duro y sólido peñasco,
> De christalinas aguas bien cercado,
> Viéredeis una Tuna estar plantada,
> Y sobre cuias gruessas y anchas hojas
> Una Aguila caudal bella, disforme,
> Con braveza cebando se estuviere
> En una gran culebra que a sus garras
> Veréys que está rebuelta y bien assida,
> Que allí quiere se funde y se lebante
> La metropolí alta y generosa
> Del poderoso estado señalado,
> Al qual expresamente manda
> Que México Tenuchtitlán se ponga.
> Y con aquesta insignia memorable ...
> nuevos blasones los escudos. (2.98–112)

(Where on a hard and solid rock / Girded by crystalline waters / A cactus planted you shall see / Upon whose thick and spreading branches / A beautiful eagle sits, quite enormous, / And it will be feasting / On a great snake that in its claws, / As you shall see, is twisting, but gripped. / And here it is willed that you shall found and build / A metropolis, lofty and noble, / Of that powerful nation, well known, / And which is expressly ordered / That México Tenochtitlán it be called / And that henceforth your shields be emblazoned with that image.)

This metropolis offers a vision of the Aztec founding of Tenochtitlán, famous in Mexico today as the mythic origin of that nation. The eagle, the cactus, the serpent: these are the dream figures that, until seen in the light of day at the edge of a great lake, drove the priests and Mejica people in unrelenting pilgrimage to satisfy Huitzilopochtli. Villagrá shifts his point of geographical focus from Tenochtitlán to the cities in classical antiquity before circling back to the Americas and, finally, to la nueva México. By linking the Aztec capital to Troy, Carthage, and Rome, the Spanish writer memorializes the very pre-Columbian world he and other Spaniards continued to destroy. In a further irony, Villagrá's imperial gesture also presciently envisions what would become the national symbol of Mexican independence from Spain some two centuries later: we find that very eagle, fierce, sitting on a cactus with a serpent in its talons, today on the Mexican flag. This is uncanny when we remember that this is 1610, very early in Spanish colonial control of Mexico.

It is as though Villagrá, the criollo born in Puebla and writing in Spain, opens his epic only to whisper disaffiliation with the haughty attitude that had made him another colonial subject of Spain's vast dominion. Even if one were to argue that the Aztec figures he dresses in European clothes allow him to exploit indigenous myth to boast of Spanish conquest, a careful reading of these first two cantos discloses his fascination with and emerging attachment to the archetypal indigenous figures of his birthplace. Spain as mother country and as patria momentarily blurs in the criollo imagination. The *Historia* reflects the extent to which Villagrá's displacement from Spain—his birth in the Americas—gives way to a new cultural genealogy that is nascent, ambivalent, and conflicted but thus alive to new meaning.

Villagrá closes the second canto of the *Historia* with a sustained meditation on the complex origins of Mexico's native people as themselves immigrants from those lands far to the north we know as la nueva México and to parts of the globe unmapped. Though his retelling of the migration narrative focuses on the Mejica who settled Tenochtitlán and whose cultural story we hear, Villagrá is attentive to the complexities of vastly different native groups: "Gran suma de naciones diferentes, / En lenguas, leies, ritos y costumbres / Los unos muy distintos de los otros" (2.216–18) (A great many nations, different / In languages, laws, rituals, and customs, / All very distinct from the others). He even ventures to theorize an anthropology of native origins as the result of a much earlier and longer migration from Asia: "Que para mí yo tengo que salieron / De la gran China todos lo que habitan / Lo que llamamos Indias." (2.297–99) (For myself, I think that they did come / From the great China, all who live /

In what we call the Indies). Everyone in la nueva México has come from distant shores.

When I considered how Villagrá combined these European and indigenous Mexican figures, rituals, and origin stories into a single tale, I discovered a convergence between the old world and the new that startled me into rethinking Villagrá's aesthetic, and his political intention. Initially I had thought there was something awkward in the way Villagrá yoked Spanish "infanticos inocentes" (1.153) and "damas, dueñas y donzellas" (1. 158) with indigenous warriors dressed in leopard skins who carried "thick clubs with heavy stones / imbedded in their strong wood" (1.195–96), all of them marching through his narrative without a care ("marchando con descuido," 1.215). But the closer I looked at his phrasing and his use of multiple cultural and transcultural sources—Sahagún's Aztec pictorial manuscripts of ornately dressed Aztecas together with figures from a European masque, native origin myths together with Roman foundational myths, the story of the witch-seer in Lucan's *Pharsalia* together with Aztec priests-seers—the more it became apparent that what we are witnessing in the *Historia* is a conscious, deliberate *mestizaje* rather than a careless jumbling together of diverse source materials.

María Herrera-Sobek reads this "syncretization process" as Villagrá's way of making "the inaccessible accessible in his epic through rhetorical strategies that link European entities with Aztec ones." This, she argues, is primarily because Villagrá was "addressing a European public which was not knowledgeable about America."[25] As usual, Herrera-Sobek is on to something crucial. On the one hand, Villagrá addresses a seventeenth-century Spanish audience and appeals to their literary, cultural, religious, and political sympathies; on the other, this criollo, who writes about the Americas as a participant in the Oñate expedition, born not only in but into the new world, speaks a syncretic discourse that partially blurs the lines between the imaginations of the old and new worlds. Taking Herrera-Sobek's insight to the next logical step brings us to what I will call aesthetic mestizaje, or a poetics of transculturation. Despite postcolonial critique of his work, Villagrá's view of native people is not monologic—the theoretically clichéd notion of the indio as "Other"—but is rather the multifaceted articulation of a New World subject born to cultural difference and indigenous complexity. Though we may not want to, we must recognize in Villagrá's poetry an embryonic mestizo subjectivity.

The ideological ambivalence that surfaces in the poem must have been odd and uncomfortable for Villagrá himself. Unless we think he was simply stupid—a ruined prisoner of the rhetoric of empire—how could we believe that he wrote more than twelve thousand lines of densely allusive and intertextual poetry without feeling pressed to think about the conflicting motives governing him as a soldier of empire (disciplined and obedient to command), a writer for the King, and a poet steeped in the classics, recasting his soldiering experience in the expedition in ways that edged toward chagrin and doubt? Bringing the humanist learning he had absorbed from his studies in Salamanca into the poem would as much as require the skeptical turn of mind characteristic of the Greek and Roman authors he had read decades earlier and that were circulating in the Spain to which he returned in 1605. Yes, Villagrá might dedicate his poem to the King in order to win court favor and at the same time encode a sequence of complex questions about personal experience, culture, and nation within this poem of thirty-four cantos. If he read Quintilian, a prominent Spanish Roman rhetorician whose *Institutio Oratoria* was commonly memorized by students during the Renaissance, Villagrá would have learned how to scribe competing claims within his text, for as Quintilian noted, "Through a certain innuendo we intend something unspoken to be communicated not as an opposite, as in 'irony,' but some 'other' meaning which lies hidden ... [and] is used ... if speaking openly is unsafe [or] if doing so is unseemly."[26] And, indeed, for Villagrá, any competing claims about the royal court's handling of the Oñate expedition would have to be carefully scripted if he wanted to stay out of harm's way.

Villagrá may have remained steadfastly Spanish with respect to power over native people, but the ideological shift that informs his world view—he was born in Puebla de los Ángeles and not Madrid—seeps into his poem. In him, the criollo's emerging sense of time and space, of geographic migration and material culture and of knowledge and narrative, opens to an understanding that people separated by great distance are finally not so different, even though power relations enforce a disparity still in place today. Lopsided as criollismo may be toward the side of empire, this is what mestizaje looks like in an early seventeenth-century text where relations with indigenous cultures are not one-dimensional. The many peoples thrown together through a century of contact cast doubt upon a totalizing imperial imagination. Let us brook no illusion here: Spain continued its domination of the Americas and crushed countless indigenous people under the machine of empire. Yet

Villagrá articulates the criollo's skepticism about what constitutes nation. Over the course of the next two centuries this uncertainty would sharpen into the independence movements that by the end of the eighteenth century were manifest throughout South America.[27] In 1810, Padre Hidalgo's Grito de Dolores became the rallying cry for Mexican independence. Consider the modern Mexican flag with the icons of cactus, eagle, and serpent, and one is recalled to the sixteenth-century Aztec empire Villagrá scribes into a narrative poem that opens by retrieving a twelfth-century indigenous migration that, for readers today, envisions Mexico after 1810, exactly two hundred years after the *Historia* quietly appeared in Spain in 1610.

Four hundred years later, Chicano activists, writers, and scholars would revisit the Aztec migration as part of a political agenda claiming ancient origin in the American Southwest. In 1971, the California poet Alurista published a collection titled *Floricanto en Aztlán*, and the following year, Rudolfo A. Anaya incorporated the migration of the Mexicas into his classic novel *Bless Me, Ultima*. In his next novel, *Heart of Aztlán* (1976), Anaya probed the migration myth fully, symbolically locating the origins of the Aztecs in New Mexico. In 1989, with Francisco A. Lomelí, he edited a group of essays by leading scholars in the field titled *Aztlán: Essays on the Chicano Homeland*. In the 1970s, political activists even articulated El Plan Espiritual de Aztlán in a call to Chicano cultural independence premised upon a direct affiliation with the ancient Aztecas. Indeed, the term "Chicano" traces itself through a linguistic genealogy that begins with the ancient tribe of the Mejicas, whose Nahuatl name was appropriated as Chicano/xicano, an expression of political self-identification that in the 1970s sought to erase the affiliation with colonial Spain the term Hispanic connotes. Chicano is the assertion of cultural sovereignty discoverable in the space between Mexican and American and so refers to that iconic scene when the Mejicas, beholding the eagle perched on a cactus with a serpent clutched in its talons, discovered their historical identity and settled in the Valley of Mexico after their long journey from the north, from Aztlán.

~ 5 ~

Set this grand imagining of Aztec, or Mejica, northern origins in la nueva México over against the huge confusion of Oñate's camp in 1596, and the ideological anomalies in Villagrá's epic of empire come into focus. He might have juxtaposed the Spanish empire against Aztec origins to boast how an advanced civilization figuratively erased the indigenous track in its wake. Such a move would have allowed the *Historia* to rehearse Spain's glories a la Virgil or Camões. We do not, however, witness an epic vision laid before the Spanish Christians by one of the Lord's angels; learn of any saintly figure in the desert guiding the camp onward; see banners furling in the wind, bright pavilions, beautiful damsels and young knights vying with each other in chivalric contest; or even cherubic Spanish children playing in the fields. Rather Villagrá describes for us the great Spanish camp stuck in the desert for several years waiting for final permission from the Viceroy to proceed. Hundreds of people—soldiers, wives, children, mestizos, Indian servants—and thousands of horses, cattle, sheep, and goats have been gathered by Juan de Oñate, eager to begin the great journey and, in Villagra's verse, confused and dispirited.

Oñate, who put up his family wealth to underwrite the project, had enemies and competitors, all furiously trying to undermine his leadership well after he had carefully negotiated a contract with the King. Villagrá, who as a poet must have hated the task of wasting verse to detail these personal and bureaucratic intrigues, chronicles this imbroglio—unfortunately for the poetry. Cantos four through eleven are sluggish, sometimes tedious. It is as though the verse cannot breathe when Villagrá records how bureaucrats get hold of the expedition. One cannot imagine such machinations happening in the *Aeneid* or at least not in the same way. Aeneas delays not because petty officials are squabbling for power but rather because the beautiful Dido tempts him to build his country with her. Far enough removed from history to incorporate this Homeric topos of masculine will and weakness, Virgil can imagine the national origins in genuinely epic ways that Villagrá cannot. Perhaps the journey of the Aztecs is a proxy for the Spanish entrada, a kind of wishful thinking on the poet's part. Perhaps, when writing the *Historia* in the years after 1600, he wanted to give himself fully to epic grandeur but found himself yanked back to the mundane reality of what was in essence a business enterprise for which there were competing claims, official letters granting the contract to Oñate, and other letters casting suspicion on the expedition, all confounded by the equivalent of venture capitalists warring with each other for control of the futures market.[28] Such petty, divisive realities damage the imagination and nearly sink the poem. Villagrá must have felt this sluggishness when reading through his drafts; nonetheless, he turns this nearly intractable material into a critique of the corrupt bumbling of those in charge. This long section of verse chronicle, however, offers some relief in the writer's effort to memorialize the common settlers in Oñate's camp. Villagrá unsparingly exposes the illusion of imperial coherence by describing the frenzy for plunder, for titles, for land by desperate and mostly poor settlers who, having little, have everything to lose. The muster rolls disclose that people, Villagrá among them, put up everything they owned as collateral for being allowed to join the expedition.

Villagrá's rhetorical strategy presents both him and us with a dilemma: the chronicle weighs the poetry down, but by focusing on the mundane and the politically unpalatable, Villagrá seems to be experimenting with a verse realism that radically shifts away from the chivalric romance still popular in the early seventeenth century and that was quashed by Cervantes's assault on that genre. It seems to me that Villagrá participates in this move toward realism by elucidating the fears and feelings of the many soldier-settlers who suspected the King and Viceroy were exploiting them. In cantos six through eleven, Villagrá traces the hardships of ordinary people struggling to maintain faith in their decision to invest their life savings in a gamble for wealth, land, and, however absurd for contemporary readers, titles of respect.[29] These cantos chronicle the mundane, but they do so in a voice that respects the lives of common people, whose experience can never be the material of epic poetry—a genre typically dedicated to honoring the lives of the powerful. In classical epic, the grief and frustrations of common people are voiced to provide the enterprising hero—Odysseus or Aeneas—a dilemma to be overcome that will increase his and the nation's fame. In Villagrá the people's fear and confusion are a bit ameliorated by Oñate, who deceives them into staying with the expedition lest he lose the contract and his huge investment.

Villagrá uses these early cantos both to relate what seemed an interminable delay and recount a history of sixteenth-century ventures into the vast northern regions of New Spain, which in his poem serve as fables of failure. By focusing upon the expedition's initial missteps and political intrigues, he effectively represents (in retrospect) its ultimate breakdown—not unlike many earlier expeditions with similar aims that had laughably failed. Appropriately, he opens by describing Álvar Núñez Cabeza de Vaca's (1527–36) long trek across what is now Texas and southern New Mexico with a small band of fellow Spanish stragglers who had been shipwrecked off the coast of Florida, and who over some seven years walked back to Mexico, charting a cognitive map as they made their way. Cabeza de Vaca's stories of their journey among various native peoples, which hinted at a great city and shimmering gold just beyond the western horizon, set off a frenzy of competition for rights to explore and exploit the far north.[30] Within a few years, an expedition of several thousand Spaniards and their Indian retainers ventured from central Mexico in search of riches, whether in gold or Indian labor. In the third canto, Villagrá charts this vast entrada, which the wealthy young Francisco de Coronado led. He writes of the Coronado expedition, imagining not heroic exploits but focusing on the wholesale demoralization the soldiers felt, an alienation that led most of them to desert the expedition when the land proved sparse and its inhabitants poor (3.334–38). On the one hand, Villagrá the soldier has little sympathy for the Coronado explorers, who knew the perils of the long journey, he insists, and should have displayed greater resolve; on the other, Villagrá the poet exposes a vision fueled by greed and naivety. About the fiasco that concludes this expedition he writes with pure disdain both for the soldiers and the premise of the expedition itself: "Porque como no entraron tropezando / Con muchas barras de oro y fina plata, / Y como vieron que las claras fuentes / Arroyos y lagunas no vertían / Dorados sopas, tortas y rellenos, / Dieron todos en maldezir la tierra" (Because they had not stumbled / O'er bars of gold and fine silver / And when they saw that the clear waters, / Arroyos, and ponds did not pour out / Gilded soups, tortas and rellenos / They all took to cursing the land) (3.449–54).[31]

Succeeding cantos in this early section chronicle the failed journeys of Francisco Chamuscado with a group of Franciscans in 1581, the expedition of Antonio de Espejo (1582–83), and then two unauthorized expeditions by Gaspar Castaño de Sosa (1589) and then Bonilla and Humaña (1593). This portion of the poem closes with a long stanza detailing the unauthorized expeditions, all of which the Viceroy severely punished, but all of which nevertheless fueled a poisonous hydra ("hydra ponzoñosa") among "hombres valerosos" that turned them into venomous dogs ("perra venenosa," 5.250–61). There is no Homeric sublime here. The grit of desert sand produces a mirage that sent Spaniards into a ravenous frenzy ("gran rabia") that Villagrá bemoans as a "gota coral, furioso" (furious epilepsy) and a "beneno mortal" (fatal poison).

When he finally turns to describing how the King and Viceroy chose Juan de Oñate to lead the great expedition, all these preceding tales of greed and failure color what should be a boast. We read a few cantos in which Oñate's image is plumped, partly by reference to his New World royal mestizo genealogy in which Moctezuma's and Cortés's blood mingles in the Oñate clan and then by comparisons of Oñate to classical figures that confer a certain heroic stature. Yet, the cantos here operate by both analepses and prolepses, tales that flashback to earlier failed entradas and shadow Oñate's own grand entrada, by 1610 just another doomed vision. It is no surprise, then, that in the ninth canto we find the Oñate camp stagnating for more than a year and on the verge of collapse. The colonists are tired of waiting, angry and already demoralized before they have ventured a league north. Even the livestock wander off by the thousands across the desert, an event that occasions an episode of mock epic humor:

> Y aquesta desventura fue tan grande
> Que andaban a millares los corderos
> Balando por sus madres, que perdidas
> Balaban assimismo por hallarlos,
> Y atónitas las yeguas, discurriendo
> Cruzaban por los campos sin sentido
> En busca de sus crías relinchando,
> Y assimismo las vacas y terneras
> Hundían con bramidos las campañas,
> Los tiernos rezentales, assombrados,
> Con el ganado prieto yban rebueltos
> Por verse de las cabras divididos.
> Los bueies, los caballos, los jumentos,
> El ganado vacuno y la mulada,
> Con todo lo demás que el campo pasta,
> Esparramados todos y perdidos
> A su albedrío y sin orden alguna
> Andaban sin sus guardas descarriados.
> Y sin mirar aquesta desventura
> Y perdida, sin traza, desdichada,
> Vuestro visitador mandó tras desto
> Que todos los soldados y oficiales
> O gente de servicio que quiesse
> Dexar de proseguir aquesa entrada
> Que todos libremente se quedasen
> Aunque alistados todos estuviessen. (9.215–40)

(The misadventure was so great / That lambs by the thousands wandered there / Bleating for their mothers, who, / Lost too, were bleating loudly to find them, / And mares, quite bewildered, went scurrying / And running through the fields aimlessly, / Neighing in search of their colts, / And likewise cows and heifers / Filled the fields with bellowing, / While tender, frightened calves / Were carried off with porcine herds, / Seeing themselves divided from the goats. / The oxen, the horses, asses / The cattle, and the herd of mules, / With all the rest that crops the grass, / All widely spread and lost, / At their own will and with no order roamed, / All strayed without their guards. / And, disregarding this calamity / And loss, anarchic, unfortunate, / Your inspector did order after this / That all the soldiers and the officers / Or serving folk who well might wish / To cease continuing with this expedition / Might freely then depart / Although all enlisted there.)

This is pure parody, but parody deadly serious about anarchy. We are made witness to the disequilibrium created when the state is so fractured that its subjects—human and animal alike—lapse into anarchy. Villagrá compromises poetry so as to report not that the gods are arguing over the fate of men but that the Viceroy's official inspector is bent on dismantling the expedition before it begins. The language throughout cantos seven, nine, and ten is stiff, a series of beleaguered reports in verse chronicling the Viceroy's constant efforts to undermine the journey. Yet, Villagrá turns mundane chronicle to historical fable and political allegory that function as critique aimed obliquely at King and court. The vision of livestock fleeing into the desert conveys implicit, but scalding, criticism of the King: "Que aquesto es lo que vale quando lejos / Estáis, inmenso Rey, de lo que passa" (for this is what happens, Oh mighty King, when you are so far removed from events) (9.263–64). From an imagined vantage at the edge of the Spanish empire, Villagrá impugns regal authority, careful, of course, to separate the King from his incompetent minions. The failure of the King's word, or cedula, to carry force here at the ends of the earth—the global terrain that belonged to Spain in the sixteenth and seventeenth centuries—cannot but foreshadow a kingdom spinning out of control. As he was completing the poem in Spain in 1610, Villagrá would have known that the royal coffers were empty, that the wars in Europe had already vastly depleted the nation, and that the Americas were regarded merely as a potential bank for paying off Spain's huge debt. By parodying the political intrigues besetting the Oñate expedition, a small and remote enterprise inching along at the end of the sixteenth century, Villagrá's *Historia* offers a guarded meditation on the impending failure of empire.

Reading the broad opening sweep of the poem four hundred years later, it is impossible to imagine this epic serving as a narrative model for the imperial statuary at the Albuquerque Museum.

CHAPTER 2

La Colonia
THE UNSETTLED FIRST SETTLEMENT

En este medio tiempo, unos soldados	At about this time, some of the soldiers,
Amotinando el campo, fuero preso,	Inciting mutiny within the camp, were seized,
... por cuia causa,	... and for this reason
Queriendo el General hazer castigo,	The General wanted to execute them,
Fueron tanto aquéllos que cargaron	But there were so many who begged
Con lágrimas, lamentos y con ruegos,	With tears, lamenting, and with prayers
Que general perdón allí alcanzaron.	That they were given a general pardon.
Por cuia causa, todos consolados,	And for this reason, with everyone consoled,
Por sólo aqueste hecho se ordenaron	For this reason alone there was ordered
Unas solemnas fiestas que turaron	A solemn fiesta that lasted
Una semana entera, donde ubo	An entire week, during which
Iuego de cañas, toros y sortija	Jousting with cane spears, bullfights, tilting
Y una alegre comedia bien compuesta,	And a drama well-written and lively,
Regozijos de moros y Cristianos,	The delighting "Moors and Christians"
Con mucho artillería, cuio estruendo	With thunderous artillery, whose roar
Causó notable espanto y maravilla	Stirred great fear and wonder
A muchos bravos bárbaros que abian	To many bold barbarians who had
Venido por espías a espiarnos.	Come there as spies to spy on us.

(*Historia de la Nueva Mexico*, 16.92–109)

Juan de Oñate se llamaba. Este hombre	Juan de Oñate was his name, a man
Era valiente y un gran conquistador.	Who was courageous, a great conquistador.
Hombres muy fieles, fueron sus caballeros	His soldiers were very loyal men.
Era en Julio mil quinientos noventa y ocho	In July of fifteen hundred and ninety-eight

Que completaron su larga expedición.	They set out on their grand expedition.
El río grande lo siguieron rumbo al norte	They followed the Rio Grande north
Cuando llegaron a ese pueblo de San Juan.	Until they reached the pueblo of San Juan.
En Yunque-Yunque con toda su belleza	And in Yunque-Yunque with all its beauty
Establecieron la primera capital.	They established the first capital.
En este tiempo empezó todo la historia	And that is when the history
De Juan de Oñate primer gobernador	Of Juan de Oñate, the first governor, began.
Y cada año celebramos nuestra herencia	So every year we celebrate our hertiage
Y acordamos todos a Don Juan.	And we all remember Don Juan.
Le dedicamos nuestras fiestas en su nombre	We dedicate our fiestas in his name
Y conservamos esta bella tradición.	And preserve this beautiful tradition.
Este es un corrido muy merecido	This is a well-deserved corrido for
A un hombre querido por toda la región	A man loved throughout the region
¡Viva Oñate! ¡Viva Oñate!	Viva Oñate! Viva Oñate!
¡Viva la historia de este gran señor!	Long live the story of this great man!

("El Corrido de Juan de Oñate," 1996)

The Española Fiesta celebrates the marriage of Native American and Spanish cultures that began July 11, 1598 where the San Juan River meets the Rio Grande near the San Juan Pueblo, at a place they called yunque-yunque.

In order to insure success and continuity in the celebration known as the Española Fiesta, or Fiesta de Española, where the Fiesta celebrates the original settlement by Spanish Europeans at Ohkay Owingeh (San Juan Pueblo) where the planting of many social seeds took place that have existed and grown since July 11 of 1598 and where a marriage of two cultures took place and have created a unique culture. And, although struggles occurred and existed the brotherhood has weathered the test of time. The Fiesta de Española honors the Spanish men and women who dared to make Nuevo Mexico their home in 1598. The fiesta honors the traditions, and heritage established by the Spanish European settlers.

(Española Fiesta Mission Statement, 2007)

Española is a city of some ninety-eight hundred people situated at the confluence of the Rio Grande and the Chama rivers in northern New Mexico, twenty-five miles north of Santa Fe and a few miles south of Ohkay Owingeh, which in 1598 had what must have been an otherworldly name bestowed, or rather forced, upon it: San Juan de los Caballeros. Four hundred years later, a confluence of names, memories, opposing histories, and realities surfaces every July when those gathered for the Española Fiesta celebrate the first Spanish colonial settlement in what is now the United States. The fiesta council mission statement narrates a version of history that would have us believe the indigenous world not only welcomed the Spanish, but also willingly forfeited their world to accommodate the new settlers and gladly entered into a "marriage" that would produce a "unique culture." I do not think the council intended any slight. The statement summarizes a long history in which Nuevomexicanos articulate their own sense of belonging and stability in a world American culture dominated after 1848. In the homespun rhetoric of hardworking people preparing their annual ritual of cultural identity we read a desire to seek kinship with indigenous people as a symbolic bulwark of permanence. Whoever on the committee wrote the statement expresses the group's sentiment that for the most part Pueblo people and the descendents of the first European settlers have moved past their differences and not only live in peaceful proximity but also, because of that long proximity, have produced a unique culture, by which the committee means a mestizo culture. Better in New Mexico to suggest mestizaje than to state it outright, as the next phrasing makes clear, where the weight of cultural identity is situated in a defensive affiliation with Spain rather than the indigenous world: "the fiesta honors the traditions, and heritage established by the Spanish European settlers."

Over the span of four centuries, "struggles occurred," but today the Española valley is represented as a "brotherhood" of mostly working-class people whose historical consciousness is embedded in an ideal of intercultural harmony. Yet this harmony, I would argue, is vested in an anomalous power equation in which working-class Chicanos, dressed as Juan de Oñate and his lieutenants in sixteenth-century regalia, ride on horseback (clop, clop, over asphalt streets) into town to claim indigenous terrain, yet again, for King and Church. "El Corrido de Juan de Oñate," which sings Oñate as "un hombre valiente," "un gran conquistador," "primer gobernador," and "un hombre muy querido," serves as a ballad complement to the statuary outside the Albuquerque Museum memorializing the Oñate expedition. The corrido, a traditional ballad form that harkens back to the medieval troubadour tradition, narrates a significant historical event, remembers a tragedy, or celebrates the exploits of a heroic figure. "El Corrido de Juan de Oñate" reproduces in song the sculpture's vision of an intrepid Oñate leading his group of settlers north, all of them carved with hopeful and steady faces, while one figure, an Indian, literally has his shoulder pressed to a cart wheel he is pushing out of a sand rut. Is this the "brotherhood" of which the council speaks?

When I think about these contemporary representations next to Gaspar Pérez de Villagrá's epic, I know that historical amnesia and its insistent fabulations have done Nuevomexicanos a tremendous disservice. The corrido is a fable that heroizes a man widely regarded as a self-serving failure in his own day. In 1610, Villagrá's poem begins to tell the truth about Juan de Oñate. Four centuries later, we glorify a man this poet exposed in the first moment of far northern empire as deceitful. Yes, New Mexico's first governor ordered "fiestas," but he did so to cover over his settlers' disillusionment with his leadership as well as to parade Spain's empire before the native people whose world it had disrupted. Today we are still bound up in ceremonials that memorialize "the original settlement by Spanish Europeans at Ohkay-Owingeh" in towns and villages throughout northern New Mexico.

I concede that at first glance Villagrá's *Historia* appears to initiate an imperial boast. Yet, well before he details the destruction of Acoma in the last third of the poem, a closer reading suggests that Villagrá, over the course of twelve thousand lines, exposes a foundation of deceit and fracture within the Spanish camp that troubles any facile reading of the epic as panegyric. Today's fiesta goers, the corrido tells us, celebrate "nuestra herencia"—our heritage—and dedicate the festivities in collective honor ("acordamos todos") of don Juan, this "gran señor." The Oñate of Villagrá's poem, by contrast, wanted to garrote his own soldiers within a week of their arrival and refrained only when the colonists were reduced to begging for lenience. The fiesta he gave them was meant to shut them up with festive distraction. "Juego de cañas, toros y sortija" (Jousting with cane spears, bullfights, tilting) would entertain them until he could consolidate his imperial authority. After reading Villagrá, it is impossible to imagine the Spanish colonists of 1598 singing along with the contemporary ballad. Rather than a "¡Viva Oñate!" one would have heard muttering. So much for celebratory verse about the settling of a harmonious Spanish community and so much for the first week-long fiesta of 1598.

Some ten years after he had left la nueva México for good, Villagrá recalls in his poem an outpost filled with misgiving. By establishing structural disaffiliation within the poem, Villagrá artfully, which is to say carefully, undermines his own earlier loyalty to Oñate, as though coming to a simmering realization that he, like the other colonists, had been duped by a wealthy despot intent on his own gain. The persona Villagrá assumes within the *Historia* remains the loyal soldier, but, because he was writing the poem some ten years later, divided and troubled by the past, its narrative structure discloses a failed venture, the vainglorious apex of which is the wanton destruction of Acoma.

Before we come to that sad portion of the *Historia*, however, we must follow the Spanish up the Rio Grande to their arrival at a "gracioso pueblo" (16.11) where they planted the flag of empire still memorialized today. The small Tewa settlement that was the unlucky host for the first Spanish settlement in 1598 is still a village but a village fiercely proud of its ancient name—Ohkay Owingeh—whose title has erased the highway signs that for so long read "San Juan Pueblo." Yet Española, the neighboring town, is by its very name a visceral reminder of that colonial encounter.

~ 4 ~

In the late summer of 1598, after a five-month trek across the vast northern desert of Mexico, Juan de Oñate, with his company of some five hundred colonists, arrived in a fertile valley nestled between two rivers and two mountain ranges, and there they promptly appropriated a Tewa village that had been settled for hundreds of years.[1] Over the course of a few months, the Spaniards did not just impose themselves upon this river valley, they explored the vast buffalo plains to the east and traveled west hundreds of miles in search of potential silver mines. Renamed San Juan de los Caballeros, Ohkay Owingeh was less a settlement than a staging area for Spanish explorers who set out to discover another city of gold or another mountain lined in silver, like the one in Zacatecas that had made the Oñate family wealthy. In this place somewhere between myth and reality, they staked their uncertain futures, hoping to discover another Tenochtitlán.

Their dreams were immediately dashed. In San Juan, as we shall call it for now, daily life produced a tight circle of anxiety and regret. No sooner had an entire train of colonists finally arrived on August 18 than there was a mutiny, when a group of soldier-colonists expressed doubt about Oñate's vision and wanted to return to Mexico. Oñate decided to execute them and relented only, Villagrá writes, when their friends and relatives begged him for mercy, "Con lágrimas, lamentos y con ruegos" (16.97) (crying, lamenting, and loud prayer). In a feigned gesture of reconciliation, Oñate first held a ceremony of atonement and then ordered up fiestas, theater, and Christian rituals to distract his settlers from their appalling sense of displacement, as well as to symbolically displace the indigenous people Spain had claimed for King and Church. As we shall see, this festive event simultaneously disclosed both the iron will of empire and its first fracture in the far northern reach of New Spain. Then as now, ritual celebrations conferred a sense of community, often disguising social fragmentation and alienation. When the festivities that grant reprieve from the labor and disparities of everyday life come to a close, the troubling realities and resentments resurface, and disillusionment, grievance, and rebellion sometime erupt.

In his representation of the first fiestas in la nueva México, Villagrá discloses how the constraints of empire quashed native people by simultaneously making them barbarians and subjugating them to the King's own loyal subjects. When we read his foundational epic today, four hundred years after its publication, we are so alert to the stain of empire in the Spanish colonial Southwest that we may fail to read a poetry of muted criticism articulated in the tropes, allusions, and structural oppositions Villagrá quietly put into operation that undermined a servile historical chronicle (as is commonly argued) with pointed ideological ambiguity. Villagrá's poem is almost always read as laudatory of empire until one notices the oddly placed references to classical figures or the discomfiture of adjoining cantos that ideologically contradict one another. While he may have scribed the first Spanish settlement of la nueva México, then, the poet of 1610 did not produce an uncritical spectacle of domination like the 1996 corrido that celebrates Juan de Oñate in the summative line: "Era valiente y un gran conquistador."

Those of us Hispanos who lay claim to a centuries-long presence in New Mexico have become subjects of another empire. This makes us sometimes nostalgic for an idea of cultural sovereignty that soothes broken egos or stands as a political symbol of cultural resistance. The ballad of Juan de Oñate serves our wayward resistance. The ballad, performed at the Española Fiesta along with a dramatic entrada, or parade, is featured on the website for the New Mexico Hispanic Culture Preservation League, a group of perhaps well-meaning cultural preservationists who wish to ensure that their contributions to the formation of the American West, especially New Mexico, be remembered as distinctly European and distinctly "first," that is, before the English settled on the eastern seaboard. As the site announces, "The mission of the New Mexico Hispanic Culture Preservation League is to preserve the heritage, Spanish language and the history of Hispanic New Mexico, to promote the education and understanding of the contributions of Hispanics to the development of New Mexico and the nation, to protect the history of the New Mexican Hispanic heritage and culture." The league goes on to claim: "Our ancestors were prime movers in New Mexico's history. It is sad that we did not learn that in school. Now we, and our children, have a chance to learn of our connection to New Mexico, and others will receive a better understanding of our place in United States history."[2] This narrative speaks to the historical lacunae Nuevomexicanos often feel in their own cultural world. While it is indeed crucial to have a historical sense of one's place in the world, however, the stories about the past we venerate are sometimes illusory.

When we celebrate the Spanish colonial past, we are actually resisting the American intrusion of 1848. We have been here longer: "Our roots are here," we tell others and ourselves, "not on your East Coast"; we see the world differently; we have our own cultural practices and traditions; here our sense of the future is connected with our long past.[3] Overcompensation is often the result, such that the fiction of empire too often blinds us to the long memory of the native groups we displaced here. The fiesta council's acknowledgement of mestizaje—"a marriage of two cultures"—is indeed real in the history of people in this river valley, though it bespeaks a complex history of proximity and unequal power relations, muted now that hispano and indio both live in the United States.

Perhaps I can offer myself as emblem of such overcompensation. When I was a boy growing up in Albuquerque's South Valley, what I knew of my own cultural history can best be described, I suppose, as a kind of unconscious Spanish colonial residue mixed with a lesser sense that we were also Mexican. This is not because we had studied Spanish colonial history or Mexican history of the Southwest in school, for like other American schoolchildren we were told that our national antecedents were the gray Pilgrims who landed at Plymouth Rock. The cultural preservationists have that part of the story right. Although I did not glimpse Villagrá's *Historia de la Nueva Mexico* until two decades ago, people sometimes mentioned a poem about our land that had been written many centuries before. This did not surprise me since family had told me that we were here before the English. Still, we usually thought of ourselves as American kids, at least until an Anglo reminded us that we were "just Mexicans." Although most of the Nuevomexicanos I grew up with did not have immediate family roots in the Mexico that shaped the modern Southwest, especially after 1900, they were comfortable referring to their language as "mexicano," relaxed with a son-in-law from Sonora, at ease traversing the border region. All the same, we felt different. I vaguely knew that our people had been in New Mexico for "a long time," as my Grandma López would say. My mother Esperanza still refers to this long-settled place as nothing less than her spiritual country—"mi país"—a site, that is, within neither the United States nor Mexico. This was family history, an unofficial form of cultural history that fused genealogy with a keen sense of long habitation in this spare geography.

Both my maternal grandma Josefita and my grandpa Salvador were born in northern New Mexico, he in Ojo Caliente some twenty miles northwest of Española, she in the Tierra Amarilla area. They were second cousins: families from tiny villages twined closely, not to exclude, but simply to survive into the future. The interrelationships are even more pronounced on my father's side: my grandpa Melitón and grandma Regina, I learned to my shock, were also cousins. The Padilla family dates back to the Merced de los Padillas (a land parcel Spain granted) of the early eighteenth century and, as I recently learned, my own paternal strand emerges from an ancestor, Esteban Padilla, who was the illegitimate son of the land-grant patriarch Diego de Padilla and one of his Indian servants. Of course, this mestizo son was excluded from the official family rolls until he insisted his presence back into the Padilla clan when, piecemeal, he bartered cash for land from his half-siblings. He and his wife, Jacinta, also mestiza, had ten children, all of whose baptismal records list them as *coyotes* or mestizos. So much for the fantasy of *pureza de sangre* in my Padilla family![4] Given this family history, I must disassociate myself from the puerile claims of the Spanish preservationists whose nostalgia for a conquistador cultural genealogy reproduces an ethnocentrism I find socially and politically repugnant. This is all the more so when my reading of Villagrá's epic suggests that he struggled with empire's destructive machinery in a poem that narrates colonial domination while disclosing his own guarded aesthetic disaffiliation from Oñate and Spain.

Since this chapter focuses on the 1598 founding of San Juan in northern New Mexico, I will now take us back upriver to a time centuries later when, as a child, I visited family there and learned that my mother's side had deep memory there. In those long-ago summers, we sometimes drove to Chamita, a village on the western edge of Española adjoining Ohkay Owingeh, to visit cousins on my mother's side. Memory: the embrace of mother's and grandmother's stories; the questions I asked on the long ride in the heat of summer with my eyes wide to the confluence of the Rio Grande and the Rio Chama, driving through "San Juan Pueblo"; going to mass in the mission church, then quietly standing in the shade to watch the people dance their age-old summer solstice dances. Later in the day, back in Chamita, I walked with my cousins. I remember wide fields of alfalfa and corn sloping down to the Chama River, fruit trees, the thick cottonwood bosque, and homes that all looked about the same: tin roofs, some, and others flat Pueblo style but simple, many with outdoor privies and all with wood-burning stoves. Old Fords that still ran were parked alongside Buicks that had not worked for years from which one could pull spark wires or fuel pumps or hoses for cars that took people to their jobs or to Española for groceries. Like so many rural Nuevomexicanos, my *prima* Isabel recently sold her family home and some property in Chamita and moved to Albuquerque, where I grew up. Back then, though, we stayed at the home of Isabel's parents, Santiago and Andreita, which I remember as a tin-roofed adobe with very thick doorways. Years later I would see photographs of such houses in fancy coffee table books that described these homes as classic northern New Mexico "adobes" that kept the heat in during the winter and stayed cool during the grueling summer. As I recall, my prima's house was already old, and it echoed with the sound of voices, the bang of iron skillets, and, at night, the creaking of doors and heavy wood beams. What I remember best is walking down to the Chama River to fish, catching more carp than trout, wading in the cool, silty water, sitting in the shade of massive cottonwoods. Benji, my cousin, a reddish-haired tough, would ask what Albuquerque was like and "could I go stay with you?" Now I think of the irony of my lazy comfort along the river in a place where there were more hills and trees and water than in the "big city," while he, tired of Chamita's simple life and edging toward adolescence, imagined pretty girls and "cool rides" and "more stuff to do" somewhere else.

In those long moments of summer childhood, the future waiting, there was no press of the past, no unsettled history, no ghosts of my ancestors or theirs to menace. I do not think many of us really understood that way back in the summer of 1598 our cultural ancestors *made* themselves at home here along the river in another cultural universe. The "Spanish conquest," as it was termed in the history books, was residual by the time I was a boy, dust on the ledges and dimming words that lined historical markers on highways across the state that I never stopped to read until I was an adult. It was the *americanos* and the Hispano elite who celebrated the Spanish arrival. Most of "the regular people," as aunt Tina would say, "were just minding their own business, working, raising kids. Who cared if they were Spanish or indios, or whatever"—by which she meant mestizo. Our family had indeed settled in that confluence of two rivers, and it is clear to me now that there was an equal confluence of cultures in our family. My great-uncle, Tony, was a teacher and administrator in the San Juan school district and lived in the pueblo for a time. My prima tells me that kids from San Juan and Santa Clara pueblos went to Española high school with the "Spanish" kids. There are Hispano villages and native pueblos intertwined up and down the river—Taos and Ranchos, Alcalde and Ohkay Owingeh and Española, Santa Ana and Bernalillo, Isleta and Los Padillas—where our peoples have lived in close proximity for centuries but not without lines of cultural demarcation. Yet, whether Hispano or Pueblo or both, the men from the Española area farmed for a living or worked as service employees in the federal labs in Los Alamos, on road crews, in construction, or at menial jobs in Santa Fe. Some of the "Spanish" girls who took typing in high school worked as secretaries. My mother studied cosmetology at El Rito Normal College and then worked in the beauty parlor at the famous La Fonda Hotel in Santa Fe. As the fiesta promotional tells it, over their four hundred years of contact, people indeed had figured out how to live with one another. As elsewhere, they mixed and married, making mestizaje real over the centuries. To echo the fiesta council blurb: "a marriage of two cultures took place and created a unique culture. And although struggles occurred and existed the brotherhood has weathered the test of time."

Yet this is romance as well. What I did not realize as a kid was that there must have been simmering memories of 1598 in the minds and hearts of Pueblo kids who were also gazing into the Rio Grande—its Tewa name unknown to me but steady in their universe of words—during those same summer days. These kids would grow up to courageously recuperate their tribal history, one day taking down the "San Juan Pueblo" signs, proclaiming their own heroic past in the figure of

Po'pay, the Ohkay Owingeh spiritual leader who strategized the 1680 Pueblo rebellion against the Spanish invaders. I now understand that the stories their parents told them must have recalled an ancient intrusion in which their river valley filled with hundreds of oddly dressed people and thousands of strange animals stomping across their fields. Strangest—and most galling of all—must have been the stories of watching all these stragglers in their village, day after day, occupying already small spaces, gathering Ohkay Owingeh corn at harvest, pillaging their blankets when first snow fell. Po'pay was born to this story of displacement and humiliation decades after Oñate had been deposed. The Española Fiesta narrative does not tell this story, except perhaps in the subscripted meaning of the phrase "struggles existed." Struggles exist here today in yet another empire.

On Monday, when the fiesta booths have come down, the people go back to their daily lives, the town returns to the present and to struggles that implicate everyone in a corporate economy that has little interest in local histories, however old and complicated. Today, when you drive through Española you see a crosssection of American small towns, local businesses fighting to hold on against the corporate giants that grid every small town and city across the country. There is El Rey Discount Liquor, Joanne's Restaurant: Native New Mexican Food, J. T.'s Secondhand Furniture Store, Los Cucos Restaurant. Then, inevitably, there is Wal-Mart, Burger King, Walgreen's, H&R Block, Pizza Hut, Radio Shack, Wells Fargo Bank, and, needless to say, McDonald's.

What is new but forever old, however, is the large casino some four miles north of Española on the road to Taos that four centuries after the first encounter still holds the promise of quick riches. This fantasy place is Indian owned, however. The Ohkay Casino and Resort Hotel sits on a stretch of road east of the pueblo, and from the parking lot you behold the soft-shaped Sangre de Cristo mountain range, ski trails carved out of dark green mountainsides that once were all pine and aspen. When you walk into the casino from out of the Española heat in July, the floor is refrigerated and dimly lit, except for the slots, a rainbow of lights, going and going and going with the sound of spinning, the clinking of nickels or quarters falling into slot troughs when the digital numbers or clown faces or pirate ships line up. The casino has a good bar where happy hour buys a cold Budweiser tall neck for $1.20 and well drinks for a buck-fifty. There is the typical casino buffet, which on a Friday evening brings the ocean to the high desert with king crab legs, mounds of shrimp on ice, baked salmon and herring, and—hard to believe—fresh oysters on the half-shell. On Friday and Saturday nights the bar becomes a nightclub where local couples and singles dance Latin *cumbias*, the western two-step, New Mexico style *rancheras*, and golden oldies, and where between sets the singles in their twenties dance sharp-angled and erotic hip-hop to disco. Pueblo couples dance next to young Chicano couples, next to cowboys, next to mixed groups of young women who, mostly, just want to dance—not get lied to by hungry-looking guys in their thirties drinking beer at the long bar.

The casino floor is filled with people sitting at the slots. They are intense and determined: middle-aged women with cigarettes welded to their lips; young guys just off shift and still wearing name-tagged shirts: "Eddie," "Lefty," "Al"; senior citizens who do not need to ask a granddaughter for a ride because the shuttle picks them up at "the center." These gamblers are mostly Chicanos—"Hispanics," as we are officially called now—or, as many of the older folks still call themselves, "Spanish"—but they are mostly working people living in small houses or trailers for whom this entertainment offers the same illusion that a win against long odds will change everything. Theirs is much the same jackpot their cultural ancestors hoped to win when in 1598 they packed their meager belongings in a wager with a wealthy silver miner from Zacatecas who had won the King's contract to explore a region far to the north that, against all evidence and reason, offered the same illusory glimmer of wealth en una nueva México.

~ 2 ~

Gaspar Pérez de Villagrá's epic poem narrates a late sixteenth-century gamble by the Spanish equivalent of today's working-class people sitting at the slots of the Ohkay Casino Resort and Hotel. The people who came with Juan de Oñate were generally of limited means, people who, like Villagrá, had invested their own property and cash in the venture.[5] Those who came across the ocean were mostly from small, desperate villages, people driven by images of a gilded New World. They had squirreled just enough money to leave a country that ruled that world but, as usual with empire, crushed its own peasants. They made their way to the Americas from towns in Andalucía, Extremadura, Castilla-León, Castilla de la Mancha. Others from las Canarias and Portugal joined the expedition as well. Almost all, however, were criollos, mestizos, and Tlascalan Indians born in Jalisco, Guanajuato, Zacatecas, Puebla, or Mexico City. Their names remain common in New

Mexico: Castillo, Chávez, Durán, García, López, Lucero, Martínez, Montoya, Pérez, Romero, Sánchez, Truxillo, Vaca (Baca).[6]

It does not take a great deal of historical verification or imagination to envision people in the late sixteenth century risking their savings to strike it rich in Nueva España. Theirs was a last-ditch toss of the dice in what was promoted as another Tenochtitlán that would yield that precious, lovely, and killing metal, gold, or, its silver consolation. What the *Historia de la Nueva Mexico* bequeaths to us in the present should be a reminder of regional social formations that began the moment the Oñate expedition halted at the confluence of the Rio Grande and Chama rivers.

Villagrá's poem, in the reading of that first moment I now offer, does not provide imperial boast but instead charts a history of crosspurpose, confusion, and failure of resolve. The poet's chronicling of the expedition slows the poem, but because Oñate proves not to be the beloved hero the twentieth-century corrido fantasizes, the colonial ideal gradually devolves into the Acoma massacre at story's end. That Villagrá is writing from within the first circle of empire, however, required indirect commentary through structural anomaly. As it turns out, he learned this strategy from Virgil, whose encomium to Augustus is side-glanced with critique. Richard Thomas's reading of Virgil offers a way of reading Villagrá, too: he suggests that with Augustus as much as in the same room, the Roman poet found ways to glorify Rome while also carefully incorporating intertextual reference, historical narrative, ambiguous allusions, and speeches by the Latin natives who must suffer Aeneas's punitive measures. Thomas notes that Virgil may be said to have absorbed the rhetorician Quintillius's recommendation that "if speaking is unsafe," the poet should proceed "through a certain innuendo ... something unspoken to be communicated not as an opposite, as in 'irony,' but some 'other' meaning which lies hidden" that "will only succeed if the utterance may be understood in a different way (*aliter intelligi posit*), if the danger can be avoided by ambiguity of expression (*ambiguitate sententiae*)."[7] At the University of Salamanca where he was schooled, Villagrá would have read many of the same Greek and Roman rhetoricians who taught Virgil how to praise and yet censure power through innuendo, ambiguity of expression, and anomalous use of official documents. In the middle cantos (14–18), Villagrá relates the foundational events of the Spanish settlement as it crosses into the province of la nueva México and, as Martín-Rodríguez richly argues, produces equivocation by simultaneously weaving official, historical, dramatic, and poetic discourses into his own epic.[8]

Of course, this created a methodological dilemma for Villagrá in his self-appointed role of expedition scribe per Titus Livy, a conflict that, on the one hand, produced a history against forgetting and on the other, reconstructed the expedition within a literary form capacious enough to develop competing narratives, troubled sentiments, and fictive voices not possible in the prosaic official itinerary of the expedition. The official itinerary, as cited in Hammond and Rey's collection of documents, specifically the "Record of the Marches by the Army, 1596–98," notes that at the beginning of June 1598, "the cart train was in trouble, both on account of dissension among those in charge, and a lack of water, and the governor [who was riding with the advance expedition] had to return to them. He smoothed everything by his tact."[9] No criollo bumpkin, Villagrá would have known that the historical chronicle within the poem would be cross-referenced in scores of official documents. Carefully modulated by Villagrá, their inclusion could provide oblique commentary on what by 1610 was clearly a failed expedition to la nueva México.

Although epic is often considered a form that does not easily accommodate representation of competing voices across social stratifications, I believe that Villagrá's poem, while a commemorative verse dedicated to the King and to memorializing a colonial entrada, does indeed summon competing social and ideological positions over the course of its narration that call royal authority into question, however obliquely. It is precisely the imaginative latitude in the fiction of epic that allowed Villagrá to probe into the political intrigues that slowed the expedition in ways undisclosed in state documents. Villagrá is settling old debts right under the nose of the King, who is also the subject of his disdain. The official documents he weaves into the poem allow him to distance himself from the iron template of empire. Through them he satirizes historical representation, skewering viceregal authority in la nueva México and, by extension, King and court for their irresolution over the expedition into la nueva México. Earlier in the poem, for example, Villagrá writes that a royal courier is riding into camp "con gran priessa / Pidiendo albricias por el buen despacho / De las nuevas alegres que traía / De vuestro Visorrey" (7.216–19), with great speed for his reward at delivering the happy news from the Viceroy. The news, however, is anything but good. The Viceroy has sent a letter ordering Oñate to halt the expedition under threat of losing "the titles, patents and leadership, provisions, commissions, and other remuneration, which in the name of His Majesty, have been given to the aforesaid Don Juan de Oñate"

(67). The entire letter of August 12, 1596, is inserted like a knife into the text of the poem. Delaying the expedition for two years, it created disarray and fractured morale within the camp. Included in its entirety, together with a brief note from the King himself, the letter exposes both the Viceroy and the King for fomenting one political intrigue after another. Moreover, the officiously threatening language of empire that Villagrá copies into the poem, I believe, is meant to be glaring and disruptive, a prose smudge that unsettles poetry, an authoritarian dictum that not only delays the caravan but, years later, appears like a boil upon the skin of his verse.

As usual, Villagrá's sympathy holds with his fellow settler-soldiers, who he describes as mere pawns expected to maintain their discipline while the higher-ups self-servingly negotiate and then lie to keep them in check, as Villagrá remembers Oñate doing: "La flaca soldesca entretenida / Con uno y otro engaño dilatado / Y fuerza de palabras mal cumplidas" (8.237–39) (The already weak soldiers were kept in suspense, / with one or another long-winded deceit / and words of promise never fulfilled). The situation is so bad that Villagrá remembers "Los niños inocentes y a sus madres, / Sugetos a vivir a campo abierto / Como si fueron vestias sin abrigo" (The innocent children and their mothers / Were forced to live out in the open / As though they were beasts without shelter) (8.241–43). The disdain for authority he vented in these lines initially appears to exempt Oñate, who is likened to a "ternísssimo padre, lastimado," a loving father stoically suffering the indignities imposed upon him and heroically holding the camp together with his own resources and loans from family members. Strangely, however, Oñate is then compared to a retinue of prominent Romans Villagrá inserts into the poem primarily from Plutarch's *Parallel Lives* and Livy's *Annals*.[10] What looks like an intertextual tribute buckles under the weight of the figures Villagrá lists: "Pompey, Sulla, Marius and Lucullus, / And Julius Caesar, too" (8.107–8)—bitter rivals, brutal despots, and power-mongering dictators—monomaniacal men easy with deceit and cruel in serving their own ends. Other readers may argue that I am pushing against what, elsewhere in the canto, sounds like obsequious commemoration. My sense, though, is that as the poem unfolds, Oñate's stature, though upheld in other parts of this canto, falls into doubt precisely through his apposition to such classical figures, who must have been infamous as much as famous to an audience Villagrá knew would be familiar with Plutarch and Livy. Villagrá does not openly call Oñate deceitful or a despot, but the force of the Roman references might well have raised an eyebrow in a seventeenth-century reader, just as it caught my attention and prompted me to familiarize myself with the figures the poet all at once crowds into a canto that otherwise compliments Oñate's politic forbearance. The competing allusions are not the product of a naïve mind—an amateur poet piling literary reference upon reference without understanding their social and political implications—but the work of a poet schooled in classical rhetoric who expected informed readers to develop comparisons between the celebrated Romans and Mexico's ruling families. Like "Los Fabios, Cipiones y Metellos" (8.105) (Favii, Scipii and Metelli) to whom Villagrá alludes in the canto, families in Rome who held sway in affairs of state, the Tolosa, Ibarra, Treviño, and Oñate families had acquired great wealth and power in Mexico.[11] One is reminded that Juan de Oñate was the son of the wealthy and influential Cristóbal de Oñate and that his quest, underwritten by his relatives, was no less than to deepen the family wealth and widen their geography of power from Zacatecas to la nueva México.

Oñate's noble display of restraint in the poem is undermined by his political machinations. The figure in the poem holds the demoralized camp together with a stirring speech, but this is only to buy time so that other family members can renegotiate the contract. He had to keep up appearances, deceiving the colonists into believing that everything was moving along according to plan. The family had invested heavily in the venture and in him, so failure was out of the question for the Oñates. In 1610, Villagrá exposes the entire circle of intrigue, beginning with the King, who is reminded that the Oñates have provided him "gran suma de plata," (8.130), including the Viceroy, always figured in the poem as a self-serving ingrate, and, by implication, the extended Oñate family for whom the colonists are but a cog in the machinery of wealth, held together by "uno y otro engaño dilatado" (8.238)—one or another deceit.

This indirect poetics of ambivalence and derision, I argue, is even more sharply exemplified by Villagrá's inclusion in the *Historia* of the entire text of Oñate's "Act of Possession" that functions like a kind of dramatic soliloquy. The poet draws a scene of the caravan coming to a halt as it is about to ford the river of the North (Rio Grande) on April 30, 1598, but the moment of first arrival is disrupted by Oñate's insistence on reading the entire Act, a long and repetitious religio-juridical document that, however formulaic, tells us a great deal about Oñate himself. The structural juxtapositions in cantos fourteen and fifteen are striking; the act of possession functions as an imperial speech in which Oñate claims the territory for King,

Church, and himself, while saying little about the soldiers and colonists themselves except that they are to play their parts in ensuring the success of the venture. Villagrá begins canto fourteen with the advance party—which included him—on the verge of death after riding some fifty days in search of the river. The troop rides over "riscos y peñascos escabrosos, / Ya por muy altos médanos de arena / Tan ardiente, encendida y tan fogosa" (over cliffs and ragged looming rocks / Now over lofty dunes of sand / Blazing, burning and fiery" (14.65–68). Both men and horses are desperate for water, "Vivo fuego exalando y escupiendo / Saliva más que liga pegajosa" (Exhaling fire and spitting / Saliva more viscous than pitch) (14.96–97). When they finally find the river, the men are so thirsty they lie stretched on the river bank like toads gasping in the mud, while the horses, crazed and blind, plunge their heads into the river, drinking so much that two of them burst while two others are carried away by the current, drowning in their satisfaction of water (14.85–123). The huge caravan that slowly follows also offers the reader a scene of privation and suffering, "secas las gargantas miserables, / Los tiernos niños, hombres y mugeres / Traspassados, perdidos y abrassados (their throats miserably parched / the tender children, men and women / afflicted, ruined, quite burned up) (14.204–6). Yet no sooner do they find "safe and pleasant port" (14.266) along the river, Villagrá tells us, than Oñate sends a group of men to find a suitable place to ford the water so that he can get on with his expedition. While they are gone, Oñate orders a makeshift church built to pacify the friars, asks Captain Farfán to offer one of his dramas, and then, gathering the colonists under colorful pennants and banners, proceeds to read from the scroll of empire.[12]

Villagrá offers a record of the entire statement, "Sin corromper la letra, porque importa / Por ser del mismo General la nota" (Without skipping a letter, for it imports much / As being the statement of the General himself) (14.347–48). At first glance, Villagrá seems to be recording a momentous event. The nearly three-thousand-word statement, in all of its imperial pomposity, will, however, expose the governor and the empire in unexpected ways. Oñate's declaration opens "In the name of the most Holy Trinity . . . who governs . . . from sea to sea, from end to end" but soon turns to his personal claim of authority and ownership:

> I wish that they may know, those who now are here or in time shall be, how I, don Juan de Oñate, Governor and Captain General and Adelantado of New Mexico and of its kingdoms and provinces . . . settler and discoverer and pacificator . . . inasmuch as in virtue of the

nomination which of me was made and titles which his Majesty gives me, undoubtedly, as Governor, Captain General and Adelantado of the aforesaid kingdoms and provinces ... his Majesty approves the choice made of my person and estate, exercising and continuing my said office and now come in claim of the aforesaid kingdoms and provinces.[13]

The recitation of titles the King conferred is intended to silence Oñate's competitors and ensure that his possession of the "aforesaid kingdoms and provinces" remains unimpeachable from April 30, 1598, well into the future. The adelantado then rhetorically and legally seals his claim through imperial ventriloquism: "I wish to take possession of the land ... in the voice and name of the most Christian King, our lord, don Felipe, the Second of this name, and of his successors."[14] Empire extends far in this act of verbal transubstantiation, the King-Oñate circle of power complete "from the leaf on the mountain to the rock in the river and sands of it, and from the rock and sands of the river to the leaf of the mountain," and, together with these inanimate markers in a vast geography, entire nations of native people.[15]

Oñate's claim on indigenous people, all taken into bondage in this sweeping speech, is undermined in surrounding sections of the poem. In what reads as an event occurring just moments before Oñate's speech, Villagrá recounts how a group of Indians helps him and his four companions find a safe place to ford the river and in "a sign of peace, brought back / A great number of fresh caught fish" (14. 295–305) to feed the colonists. A few lines later, Oñate, who knows the Indians have been both peaceful and selfless, refers to the indigenous nations he now possesses as "bestial y bárbara fiereza" (bestial and barbarous in cruelty") and given to "la inhumanidad que entre estas bestiales naciónes se halla" (the inhumanity which among these bestial nations is found).[16] How could this opposition between Oñate's statement and Villagrá's own narration be unintentional? Villagrá writes that he will present the entire statement, "Sin corromper la letra, porque importa" (Without skipping a letter, for it imports / As being the statement of the General himself" (14.347–48). In order, that is, to make "en esta causa cierto escrito" (14.345), a clear record against forgetting as Livy did when writing the history of the Roman Empire, but also to hold Oñate accountable to his own words.

While the governor's imperial statement is entirely denigrating of indigenous people, Villagrá himself in the middle cantos discloses a longing for cordial relations with the indios on the equalizing ground of the open grasslands. Here nature tests everyone's resolve and survival skills. Villagrá's writing in this section at least provisionally asserts his curiosity about and respect for the natives who make their life on the llano. In these cantos, native knowledge and the technologies of hunting bring the poet to an admiration that gladdens the poem. Read as a whole, the *Historia* reconstitutes this Spaniard's sense that an incalculable way of life was destroyed at Acoma in January 1599, just months after he and other colonists had glimpsed other lifeways that might have enriched theirs. Unlike Oñate's sweeping claim that "estas bárbaras naciones con nuestro comercio y trato ... ganan en su trato político y gobierno de sus Ciudades, viviendo como gentes de razón, en pulicia y entendimiento, acrecentando sus oficios y artes mecánicas ... y ordenando discretamente el trato económico de sus familias, casas y personas" (These barbarous nations with our commerce and trade ... will improve their political affairs and governing of their cities, living like civilized people, refined and reasoning, improving their offices and mechanical arts, and discretely ordering the economic affairs of their families, homes and persons), Villagrá offers a largely different vision of these "barbarous nations," as self-sufficient, well governed, and admirable in the mechanical arts of everyday life.[17]

We first glimpse this better spirit when Villagrá describes the people the Spaniards encounter at what is now Santo Domingo, a pueblo between present-day Albuquerque and Santa Fe, where the caravan rested as it made its way north. Remember that the act of possession offers to help the "barbarous nations with our commerce and treatment [that they] may acquire and gain in their political affairs ... and [in] ordering discreetly the economic affairs of their families, houses and persons." Yet in canto fifteen, which immediately follows his incorporation of the entire proclamation, Villagrá describes a group of people who already enjoy well-ordered and dignified lives:

> Son lindos labradores por extremo.
> Ellos hilan y tejen y ellas guisan,
> Edifican y cuidan de la casa,
> Y visten de algodón vistosas mantas
> De diversos colores matizados.
> Son todos, gente llana y apacible,
> De buenos rostros, bien proporcionados,
> Rebueltos, prestos, sueltos, alentados;
> No mancos, no tullidos, no contrechos
> Mas de salud entera reforzada,
> De miembros muy bien hechos y trabados. (15.316–26)

(They are extremely skillful laborers. / The men spin and weave, the women cook / and build and take care of the house, / And wear seemly cotton mantles / Of divers colors, rich in hue / They are a plain, peaceful people / Of fine faces, all well proportioned, / Restless, quick, bold, cheerful; / None helpless, crippled or maimed / But of full and robust health / Of well-formed and harmonious limbs.) The poet, moreover, notes that "nunca han tenido, ni han usado / Ninguna borrachera ni brebaje / Con que puedan privarse de sentido" (15.329–31)—they do not make liquor and hence do not engage in the binging that deprives people of their reason—and this makes them worthy of "noble estima y excelencia." Of course, he parrots the official Church line that by "La Magestad del Cielo ya dispuestos" (15.333) (by Heaven's majesty) they are disposed to salvation, as soon as the friars displace their "supersticiosos hechizeros" (15.343) (superstitious enchanters). Yet no sooner does Villagrá mollify the censors who must approve his verse before publication than he returns to complimenting the Pueblo people for their "arte de pintura" (15.338), for being "graceful swimmers" (15.336) (lindos nadadores), and for cultivating the earth and harvesting a bountiful return of "frisol, maíz y calabaza, / Melón, y endrina rica de Castilla, / Y ubas en cantitad por los disiertos" (beans, corn and squash, melon and rich Castilian plums, and grapes grown in quantity in the wilderness) (15.346–48). This is a coherent world of lush farm valleys and rivers abounding in a wide variety of fish such that "Un solo Castellaño en un solo día" (15.364) (a single Spaniard in a single day) can catch six or more "arrobas" (15.365)—hundreds of pounds of fish. The poet describes a social order maintained without the weight of laws or kingly domination ("No tienen ley ni Rey") and without harsh punishment for "los vicios ni pecados" (vices or sins).[18] Their society appears to be premised on trust and communitarian unity, their culture one whose aesthetics of everyday life lift the spirit. It is a world that should be admired and emulated—not destroyed.

The act of possession admits no such recognition. If the native people they meet remain "barbarous nations," the King's own people are made to understand that they too remain subordinate to his will, expected to obediently "populate and pacify" the land Oñate takes in possession. Phrase rolls over phrase in rhythmic cadence, a kind of mesmerizing, dreamlike summoning of imperial acquisition that invokes the full sweep of God's presence throughout the universe, from the "heavens and earth, elements, birds and fish, animals, plants and of all creatures, spiritual and corporal, rational and irrational, from the most supreme Cherubim to the most despised ant and little butterfly."[19] All creatures great and small are made subordinate to a religio-legal template imposed upon the New World that simultaneously announces the intent to impose dominion in a strangely (and for us today, estranging) incantatory voice that, together with the theater of empire, the banners and musket shot, must have lulled the caravan of weary colonists into quiescence. Reading the act, one begins to understand the power that language has to gloss over the uncertainty and alienation simmering just beneath the surface of the colonial enterprise by people who must have been not only tired, thirsty, and hungry when they reached El Paso but also fearful and disoriented, second-guessing their own decisions to stay with the caravan as it moved across a landscape of rock and blowing sand. The language and theater of empire would hold them together in community at this spot along the river, but their resolve would evaporate as they continued trudging north, crossing the desiccated *jornada del muerto* and then doubling back over to the river corridor where Pueblo people came out to gaze at them, hoping to send them on their way after offering food, but knowing very well that, as in the past, these intruders brought deceit and destruction. By the time the caravan came to a complete and final stop in Ohkay Owingeh, the colonists, seeing a peaceful and well-laid out village much like the ones they had left behind, could no longer be gulled by another spectacle of theater nor coerced by the King's, or the Lord's, presence Oñate voiced as he read through the scroll of possession.

~ 3 ~

Remembering the final phase of the journey, Gaspar Pérez de Villagrá likens the arrival at Ohkay Owingeh to a ship sailing into a "safe and pleasant port" after being battered at sea. Here and elsewhere, the *Historia* is pervaded by seafaring metaphors.[20] After crossing the ocean to Spain in 1605, Villagrá imagined the poem's visual field by conflating his memories of the vast Atlantic with those of la nueva México's desert valleys—scores of miles wide between mountain peaks, its waves of hills rising, grass undulating like water, and sunlight, which reflecting off sand, turned to wet mirage. This imaginary juxtaposition of land and sea enriches the poem, offering a visual mimesis of classical epic, which typically plays out at sea. By summoning nautical metaphors, the Spanish poet suggests how this remote terrain produced an uncertainty that was like fear of shipwreck, for though the desert had been traversed by other Spaniards throughout the sixteenth century, it largely remained an oceanic unknown still being charted along ever-receding coastlines of the interior. Maps were still directional approximations: squiggles for rivers, an ocean imagined where Arizona begins, the misty North pushing down against what is now Colorado. In this heated desert expanse, arriving at a green valley where two rivers converged perhaps seemed as fortuitous as a ship making land for the colonists who had journeyed nearly a thousand miles in the driest time of year.

If the native people of this vast interior had in their turn adopted such nautical imagery, they might have talked of Spanish galleons harbored on a river bay that they hoped would sail away as had Coronado's army half a century earlier. Not this time. The Spanish were about to put down heavy anchor. As Villagrá writes at the opening of the sixteenth canto:

> No tiene el mundo gusto tan gustoso
> Que compararse pueda al que recibe
> La gente de una flota contrastada
> Quando, de bravos vientos combatida,
> Seguro y dulze puerto va tomando
> En sossegado albergue conozido.
> No de otra suerte todo vuestro campo,
> Al cabo de fortunas y sucesos
> Tiempo y desventuras tan pesadas
> Alegre y con gran gusto fue arribando
> Hazia un gracioso pueblo bien trazado
> A quien san Iuan por nombre le pusieron,
> Y de los Caballeros . . .
> Aquí, los Indios muy gustosos
> Con nosotros sus casas dividieron.
> Y luego que alojados y de assiento,
> Haziendo vezindad, nos assentamos (16.1–21)

(The world has no greater joy than that experienced by a battered fleet, when tossed about by roaring gales, it finds a safe and pleasant port in which to shelter. Not unlike such mariners, your camp, having for so long endured sorrow and misfortune, were joyous and in great pleasure arrived at a splendid and well-designed pueblo, which they named San Juan de los Caballeros . . . and here, the Indians gladly shared their homes with us and when all settled in we endeavored to be good neighbors [translation mine].)

What a fanciful notion! What, though, if we substitute for Villagrá's hubris a certain irony here, the arrogance of empire framed by a prior poetics that discloses the presumptions of power? While writing this scene, the poet, ever the student of classical epic, must have considered how to equate the abrupt Spanish *entrada* with a similar logic of nation building in the ancient world. Virgil's *Aeneid* provided Villagrá with a model for delineating the origins of empire in uninvited harboring, together with the contrived conceits of friendship Aeneas and Oñate offer. The Trojans are described as that "army of intruders [who] first beached their fleet on Italian shores." Notwithstanding the happy prophecy that Aeneas was destined to plant a new lineage upon their soil, the Latins refuse the Trojan vision and initiate a war of resistance. Virgil pleads with Erato, the muse of love, for words to describe what will ensue after their landing, for he must "tell of horrendous war ... of battle lines / ... all Hesperia called to arms" (7.39–49) against the Trojan invaders. He momentarily mutes this inevitable violence to report Aeneas's request for amicable welcome after the long journey through the Mediterranean: "Escaping that flood / and sailing here over many barren seas, / now all we ask is a modest resting place / for our father's gods, safe haven on your shores, / water and fresh air that's free for all to breathe. / We will never shame your kingdom, nor will your fame / be treated lightly, no, our thanks for your kind work / will never die. Nor will Italy once regret / embracing Troy in her heart" (7.261–70).

At the outset of canto sixteen, Villagrá imitates Virgil nearly line for line, not because he is naively copying his model, but because in mimicking the Roman master he reveals the Spanish "landing" as one marked by an imperial aggression that makes pretense of friendship while its "legions" stand ready to destroy other cultures at first hint of resistance. By invoking the classical poetics of empire, Villagrá discloses Spain's true intent when sailing into port: namely, to own the future. Like Aeneas, who "spots an enormous wood [and] round it, birds, all kinds, haunting the riverbed and banks," and then, seeing such abundance, abruptly changes course to enter the "great shaded river, overjoyed," Villagrá imagines the Spanish delighting in the wide, lush valley between two sizeable rivers where they insist upon founding *una otra México*, unperturbed by those New World "Latins" long settled in Ohkay Owingeh as well as in the surrounding native villages.

Unlike the Trojans, however, the Spanish colonists no sooner land in "a safe and pleasant port" than they express dismay at where Oñate has led them, for the "gracioso pueblo bien trazado," however lovely and well designed, is not at all what the colonists had conjured up as they slogged across hundreds of miles of desert. The people wanted to turn right around and go home. Villagrá writes that "some of the soldiery, / Mutinying within our camp were seized (16.92–93)."[21] The ringleaders might well have been executed, but, Villagrá tells us, the colonists, "with tears, lamenting, and prayers," (16.97), begged Oñate to bestow mercy. Thus followed the appeasing fiestas with which I opened this chapter. Despite such diversions the Spanish colony was and would remain divided until Oñate was finally deposed and brought up on a list of charges his own colonists made a few years later.

Before we get to that story, though, we should examine the New World meanings of displays of power within the first New Mexico fiesta. *Moros y Cristianos*, a drama central to the idea of Spain as a nation, had been performed there for centuries as a show of cultural unity and military force against the invading Muslims, but it was first staged in la nueva México during this troubled fiesta. The 1598 performance in Ohkay Owingeh/San Juan operated on the political level in a number of ways. As Enrique R. Lamadrid eloquently writes, for "the Spanish, the archetypal antagonist and cultural other is the Moor. In the centuries-long Reconquest of Spain, mock battles between Moros and Cristianos are documented as far back as 1150 . . . In the conquest of Mexico and the Americas, the mock battles served a military and ideological purpose. *Moros y Cristianos* was regularly staged as an auto de entrada, or triumphal entry play, both for celebrations and for instilling in the Indians a proper fear of warhorses and firearms."[22] Military theater in the Americas, or as Ramón A. Gutiérrez calls them, "Spanish narratives of the conquest," staged power, here intended to scare the Ohkay Owingeh and other native people into compliance.[23] Villagrá records just such military intent poetically:

> Regozijos de moros y Cristianos
> Con mucha artillería, cuio estruendo
> Causó notable espanto y maravilla
> A muchos bravos bárbaros que abían
> Venido por espías a espiarnos. (16.105–9)

(They staged the "Moros y Cristianos" / With loud gunfire, whose roar / Created great fear and awe / Amongst the many brave Indians / Who had come to spy upon us.)

At the same time, this nationalistic drama was intended to warn the colonists against faction. The long tradition of performance would remind these Spanish subjects of their legacy of struggle against the Muslim invaders on the Iberian peninsula in the centuries after AD 711, even though they had all been born in a post-Muslim world and many of them had never even set foot in Spain. There were (and always are) proxies for the last enemy, so the colonists were being warned that self-division betrayed weakness before these New World *moros*. The well-known drama instantiated this irrational fear as the audience witnesses the Moors stealing the cross when don Eduardo, derelict in his duty, drinks too much wine and falls asleep on watch. Humiliated by Eduardo's drunken lapse as much as by Moorish bravado, the Spaniards resolve to rescue the cross, inciting a war that can succeed only if every soldier remains disciplined, "A su puesto apuntado" (Each to his appointed place) and all united "en bien acertadas filas / Marcha y batalla" (In our files well-defined, / Let us march into battle).[24] One can easily imagine Oñate squarely eyeing his soldier-colonists, warning them without a word against attempting another mutiny.

The representation of *Moros y Cristianos* also strangely prefigures the battle of Acoma, Villagrá's Virgilian language overlapping with the drama performed by the colonists in the play who insist: "Hoy sangre ha de corer, / Hoy se ha de eclipser el sol / Del humo y fuego que brotan, / De las armas del español. / Hoy no se me escapa la Turquía" (Blood shall flow before the sunset, / And the sun itself shall fade, / Clad by smoke and fiery blossoms, / From the arms of Spaniards made, / Not a Turk shall escape me).[25] The fortresslike castle where the Moors have taken the cross and barricaded themselves is not unlike the cliff stronghold from which the Acoma will taunt the Spanish a few months later and that the Spaniards will soon breach, Acoma blood bathing the sandstone cliffs, "smoke and fiery blossoms" destroying their village. The Indians at Ohkay Owingeh, including the Acoma spies, were expected to see the futility of resistance, just as Oñate expected the Spanish colonists to redouble their discipline and loyalty to cross and King.

Oñate's theater of shock and awe did not suffice for either purpose in early September of 1598. There was lingering disdain for his leadership, and within a few months Acoma would be the first pueblo to rebel against Spanish tyranny, notwithstanding the play's assurance that Spanish "brio" would squelch dissent before it erupted. In the poem, the Acoma spies who had supposedly attended the performance would report that for all the "boom," Spanish firearms were harmless; no one actually died in the dramatic altercation—or so Villagrá writes. This is epic performance, not history. That is, while Villagrá may have recalled that some of the Acoma attended the drama in San Juan, he could not have known whether they issued such a report after returning to their village. Indeed, it seems to me very unlikely that any of the Acoma were in attendance so soon after the Spanish arrived. As we will see in the next chapter, the poet dramatizes the Acoman debate about the efficacy of going to war with the Spaniards as a fiction in the machinery of classical war epic. Outside of the poem, however, we can accurately assume that for the colonists, the political didacticism of *Moros y Cristianos* fell on deaf and disillusioned ears. Most of them were not gulled or shamed into obedience by an old nationalist drama. After all, this peaceful pueblo on the banks of the Rio Grande was hardly the magnificent city of Tenochtitlán Cortés had encountered a century earlier, nor was it the Machu Picchu Pizarro conquered in 1536. There did not seem to be much at stake. Instead, they were stranded in a dusty village not unlike the ones many of them had abandoned to pursue an immense dream a world away.

Villagrá must have felt stranded as well. The epic journey he and five hundred other colonists endured did not have its commensurate reward in material gain, so the expedition offered a paltry story. In this section, the poem oscillates between chronicle and figurations of history that include the poet himself or that, more often, side-glance his presence, allowing him to comment obliquely on what took place when the expedition reached New Mexico. No sooner had the weeklong festivities ("una semana entera," 16.102) concluded, Villagrá writes, than another group of men, refusing to be pacified by Oñate's gesture, rustled a herd of horses and rode off for Mexico. With open rebellion in the ranks, Oñate sent an iron message to everyone in the new colony. He dispatched Villagrá and three other men in pursuit of the deserters with fatal orders, no matter where they should apprehend them: "Mandó el Gobernador que luego al punto / Tras dellos yo saliesse y me aprestase . . . / Y doquiera que el alcance fuesse / Que allí luego las vidas les quitase" (16.140–41, 147–48). In a politically pitched scene, the men are caught after fourteen days of hard chase, and two—Manuel Portugués and Juan González—are summarily executed. Far from San Juan, there were no neighbors to plead for trial or mercy.

Recalling the episode years later as he was writing the poem, Villagrá alludes to the Roman military practice of punishing deserters by beheading them without benefit of trial. In 1612, two years after the publication of the *Historia*, Villagrá wrote a "Justificación" for carrying out the execution that leans heavily on a military code passed down through the millennia that permits no personal feeling for execution ordered by a commander. Yet, Villagrá frames the events in such a way as to disclose the contradictions operating within the colony—and within his own heart. For while Villagrá writes of giving chase with orders to kill his fellow Christians, he simultaneously indicates that back in San Juan they were building a church (dedicated on September 8, 1599) and baptizing the children born along the journey. The structural juxtaposition seems ironic, as though Villagrá, looking back to 1598, is hinting at an early moral break in the colony that by 1600 was in shambles. While he confesses his own culpability, he distances himself emotively both from Oñate, who issued the execution order, and Torquatus, his own poetic stand-in, who is deeply aggrieved by the martial discipline he imposes:

> qual Torquato,
> Que al muy querido hijo mandó luego,
> Por transgressor del vando quebrantado
> Que la cabeza de los tristes hombros
> Allí le destroncasen y quitasen,
> Assí a los dos mandamas degollasen
> Y libres otros dos se libertaron
> Dexándonos allí la caballada. (16.150–59)

(Like Torquatus, / Who ordered that his own beloved son / As a transgressor of the broken law / Have his head from his sad shoulders / Detached and stricken off at once / So we ordered those two beheaded there, / And the other two escaped / Leaving behind the horseherd.)

On the one hand, Villagrá deflects personal responsibility by turning his readers' attention to a classic text; on the other, his gesture toward Rome teaches us a lesson in military discipline and punishment, reminding readers of the harsh expectation put before soldiers like Villagrá. He freely admits executing the two men: "a los dos mandamos degollasen." We slit their throats, he says. Oñate orders their execution, but it is the soldiers themselves, Villagrá specifically, who are charged with killing their fellow soldiers: "we ordered the two beheaded there." He carries out the general's orders, and, yet, years later, he is banished for not giving the mutineers an opportunity to answer charges before a court. The poem discloses a fatal fracture in the first moment of colonization. Mutiny must be stopped at once, else command withers. The execution in the desert was a theater of deadly coercion more threatening to the colonists than the play they enacted to frighten the Pueblo people. As adelantado and patriarch of the new Spanish settlement, Oñate was warning his charges of their obligation to him and Spain: desertion is death. Yet as Marc Simmons points out in his reading of the expedition documents, from the outset, Oñate faced challenges to his authority. His reaction was extreme: "if our reading of the piecemeal records is correct, his early difficulties had the effect of souring his mood and pushing him along a path that led eventually to suspicion of underlings, showing of favoritism, and brutal retribution meted out to those who opposed him—in short, the behavior of a natural autocrat, or even petty despot."[26] This despot is not the Torquatus to whom Villagrá alludes, however. Let me explain.

As Encinas, Rodríguez, and Sánchez note, "Manlius Imperiosus Torquatus, Roman general, had his son executed for disobeying orders."[27] Torquatus had just reinstated prior military discipline in the face of war (340 BC), mandating that no one could leave his post. When his son went in pursuit of the enemy against this order, Torquatus had him returned and, broken-hearted, had the boy publicly beheaded. Here and elsewhere, Villagrá couples the Spanish military code with that of imperial Rome. In the epic imagination, then, Villagrá is himself faithful to a code of conduct that anguishes him. One imagines from his tone that these fellow soldiers were friends, brothers in arms and "muy querido(s)"; yet, the law is iron: deserters shall have their heads cut from off their shoulders. Villagrá's allusion to the parricide of Torquatus, however, suggests that the emotional trauma created by a masculine code of conduct can rip families apart. Oñate should be Torquatus, but nowhere in the episode is the adelantado represented as burdened when he dispatches the executioners. In a clever turn of phrase, it is Villagrá who assumes the mantle of the broken-hearted Torquatus, he who honors harsh military discipline but is saddened by what he must do.

I focus here on masculine honor to emphasize the military ethos permeating the *Historia* as it relates to Villagrá's representations of the soldier-settlers he traveled with to la nueva México and who, as I have already argued, are the subjects the narrative honored. A few lines earlier, working from his rich repertoire of nautical imagery, he makes clear the danger to the entire ship of state when the "sacred anchor of obedience" ("El háncora sagrada de obediencia") is broken, "suelta, / Perdido ya el gobierno" (loose / All governing lost now) (16.129; 131–33). Yet the men who have abandoned ship are figured as "desdichados" (16.139), ill-fated or unfortunate, not shameless, but simply as having lost their way ("perdido la verguenza," 16.138). Although beheaded for desertion, the two soldiers are quietly grieved in Villagrá's phrasing of "hombros tristes"—their sad, or miserable, shoulders (without heads). What at first seems a summary historical report turns out to be suffused with troubled conscience. After all, the men were running away from what must have seemed to them Oñate's hubris and despotism. This affection is doubled, I would argue, when readers recall Villagrá's adjoining tribute to the Pueblos' system of gentler justice: "ni conozemos / Que castiguen los vicios ni pecados"— for they do not punish vices or sins (15.339–40).

The anchoring of loyalty between soldiers is powerful, figured in the historical event itself as well as in its representation years later, where the poem relates the muted but powerful story of Villagrá's own breach of duty in 1598 and then prefigures his flight from Oñate's camp in 1599. For, as it turns out, only half of Oñate's execution order was actually carried out: two of the deserters were beheaded, but the other two escaped. How can this be? Oñate ordered them all caught and executed. Having chased the deserters for fourteen days, why would Villagrá not continue his pursuit until the last two men were caught and beheaded? The poem blurs what happened. While two men are being executed, "libres otros dos se libertaron / Dexádonos allí la caballada" (16.158–59) (Two more freely escaped us / Leaving the horses behind). The 1992 translation is awkward (freely escaped us), but the Spanish syntax is also unclear. Perhaps Villagrá forgot the article "los," which would render a clearer phrasing: "los otros dos se libertaron." Maybe he purposefully mumbles the phrase. Or, perhaps in the confusion of the moment, the two *desdichados* untied themselves and seized the chance to flee. Perhaps Villagrá and his three companions were so exhausted they just gave up further chase. Or perhaps the men were let go. Whatever the case, the phrasing obscures meaning: "libres otros dos se libertaron" suggests that they had been captured, then untied ("libres") and allowed to escape ("se libertaron"). The verbal confusion here allows me to imagine that the two men were spared the Manlian injunction because they were dearer to Villagrá than the order itself. Indeed, this is the likelier scenario since, as it turns out, the two were brothers and friends of the poet.[28] Soldierly fraternity wins out over empire.

In 1614 Villagrá was charged with murder for executing the two men without a trial. The villagers in San Juan had not forgotten this cruel act, and in the list of charges against Oñate, Villagrá was also indicted. His critics contend that the entire poem was written to preempt the charges leveled against him and Oñate for both the execution and the battle at Acoma, but this has always seemed to me a shrill argument.[29] The "Justificación" he wrote in 1612 to refute the legitimacy of the charges has no justificatory complement in the poem except for the single reference to Torquatus. To insist that an epic poem of some twelve thousand lines was written solely to provide a self-justification or preempt charges leveled against him rests on a single flimsy premise—that Villagrá desperately wrote one verse line after another, measuring syllables, allusions, metaphors, classical tropes, and epic speeches, for no other than political ends and to save his own skin. This is nonsense. Villagrá left the Oñate expedition less than a year after executing the two men and helping massacre people in a native village, and over the course of the next decade he brought to poetic language events that do more to disclose than to justify culpability. The epic he labored to compose may not be a great poem and it may indeed be a poem of empire, but it is a poem that required a sustained commitment of hard work, memory, and imagination that with respect to empire opens to doubt.

~ 4 ~

Writing the *Historia de la Nueva Mexico* provided Villagrá a space for representing Spain's imperial will in the world, but, over the span of thousands of lines, he also came to terms with Spanish meanness, his people's blindness to native groups he describes as fully alive to their own place in the world, a world they had been negotiating socially, interculturally, and ecologically for centuries. A deliberate and expansive reading of the poem's internal dialectics reveals a juxtaposition of competing discourses: narrative strands that are historical chronicle, direct address to the King, doctrinal language, military code recalling Rome, all layered through Villagrá's poetic and, hence, personal musing. Return to the topos of San Juan in its early months and note that the many stories Villagrá wants his readers to imagine are all taking place simultaneously, as though the settlement, destabilized by anger, fear, and alienation, can only be understood in a poetic narrative that operates elliptically, by a strategy of multiple digression.

Of these digressions the most fascinating are those that relate the colonial encounter with native people on the equalizing ground of the llano. Here, Spanish horsemen make their way over what came to be known as the Llano Estacado: immense, grassy plains so wide and seemingly limitless they are described in the poem as oceanic, a terrain so flat the Spaniards had to mark their path by driving in pine poles (hence, "staked plains") in order to find their way back home, otherwise "if by evil chance a man were lost / Upon these plains 'twould be the same / As though he were lost and did find himself / In the midst of the sea, beyond all hope" (17.104–7).

Unlike his description of the Aztec migration myth in the opening cantos, Villagrá does not Europeanize the Plains people the Spaniards meet on what centuries later came to be called the Great Plains. While the Aztecas he fashioned were courtly, European down to their dress and manners, the Plains people are clearly a distinct culture. Villagrá, at his best, sees more fully into their humanity, their sense of humor, their well-honed skills for sustaining themselves by hunting, and their daily negotiation of life on the llano. Perhaps this is because the Aztecs he recalls from a century earlier were already figures of New World legend, whereas the people he and the colonists encounter on the llano are his contemporaries.

There are moments of what I will call a poetics of cultural rapprochement in which Villagrá, describing native people and their material practices, obliquely voices regret for having disrupted a world he had just started to understand before relations went sour. These ethnographic instances countermand the reductive narrative of Spanish callousness through which we have come to read the entire colonial period. Villagrá's poem locates itself in a world misapprehended and ravaged by his countrymen, but against this imperial stupidity he describes native people in verse that bespeaks admiration. Such a vision is only partial, unsustainable in the Spanish imagination quite simply because empire will not allow it. Villagrá's poem both portrays and exemplifies this failure. I will not argue that Villagrá engages in a confessional impulse, or worse, that he becomes a sniveling apologist for his own egregious actions. To my mind, he never concedes the military bearing of a soldier who marches into battle and accepts the death he gives. In that respect he is a warrior no less than are his antecedents in Homer's *Iliad* and Virgil's *Aeneid*. Still, a voice emerges to offer an affirming narrative of relations with native peoples that surprised me with its amplitude.

The performative assertion of empire in *Moros y Cristianos* offered a template contradicted by Villagrá's representation of the indigenous people he found in nueva México, a representation that discloses a sharp division in the Spanish sensibility. This is nowhere more evident than in the middle sections of the poem where Spaniard and Native are pictured hunting the great Llano Estacado in the same place, at the same time, and sometimes even together. While Oñate is busy shoring up his authority in San Juan, Sergeant Major Zaldívar takes a group of fifty men and travels east to the llano that reaches from central New Mexico to Kansas—that same vast stretch Francisco de Coronado traveled in 1540 seeking the fabled Seven Cities of Gold. In 1598, however, the Spaniards ride out "A descubrir la fuerza de ganados / Que los llanos de Zíbola criaban" (To find the great herds of buffalo / Which the plains of Cíbola nurtured (16.176–77). Although Villagrá was hundreds of miles south chasing the deserters at precisely this moment, the retrospective narrative is omniscient, as if he were riding with the men. This is storytelling, not chronicle, not documentary history, and it is storytelling with a moral center, a vision of what life among another people might have been like had Villagrá and his fellow Spaniards not let the national ego ruin everything. Here and elsewhere in the poem, this internal conflict oscillates within scenes that offer opposing sides of the Spanish personality, one curious and open to difference, while the other betrays a mean spirit and a flash of arrogance always ready to flare into violence.

Let us read how this works. On first venturing out onto the Llano Estacado, the Spaniards are confronted by a frightful image of "A human figure having ears / Almost half a yard long and with a snout / ... a tail / That almost dragged upon the ground" (16.190–93). It is an Indian man trying to scare off the Spaniards. They play along until the man comes into their midst, then seize him and yank off his mask, "So that, downcast, sad, and ashamed, / Weeping, he begged them to return / That muffler, which, with great laughter, / With noisy mirth and joking they gave back" (16.217–20). Next they encounter "un bárbaro gallardo / Mucho más blanco y zarco que un flamenco" (16.228–29) (a gallant barbarian / much whiter and more blue-eyed than a Fleming). This warrior with his "squadron of archers" (16.229) walks toward the Spaniards "Con grande gravedad y gran mesura" (16.233) (with great dignity and great poise) and stands before them, curious and unafraid to look at them up close. Zaldívar has one of his men approach the albino and discharge a musket next to his ear just to scare him. He does not flinch (16.190–308).

Relating stories his friends had told him, these micro-narratives are intended to be playful, for the Spaniards at least. Such intercultural levity gives the appearance of good humor toward the people they encounter, but Villagrá frames these stories to suggest that comedy emerges from power and intimidation. The sergeant who fires the musket would have known that native people were already familiar with guns and the sharp report they made. The Pueblos, after all, had been watching the Spaniards for nearly a century and undoubtedly had traded news of the invaders' theatrics of power, not to mention their brutality against the tribes in the Rio Grande valley during Coronado's march. That the white, blue-eyed Indian does not flinch, however, is a marvel ("tal prodigio") (16.248) to the sergeant, who out of respect gives him a large knife and, assuming they are now pals, asks if he can borrow one of his men as a guide to find buffalo. The guide, unwilling to be left alone with the Spaniards, runs away in the middle of the night.

We might surmise that the strangely clad figure in snout, long ears, and tail was a clown figure—a trickster who had been sent or volunteered to appear before the Spaniards in a show of defiance or burlesque.[30] Villagrá's storytelling style and tone suggest that he knew the man was poking fun at the Spaniards guised in dress no more outlandish than the heavy leather corselets, long leather boots, and strange steel helmets the soldiers wore. We cannot know for certain, of course; although Villagrá provides vivid ethnographic detail, we do not have access to native records of their encounters with the Spaniards on the llano. Despite his own cultural arrogance, though, Villagrá seems sympathetic to the plight of both native men. He tells us that the clown figure was stripped and shamed, that the albino was made the target of a cruel prank, and that the man who had been promised as a guide was rightfully distrustful of the foreigners and fled at the first opportunity. This is a not a stanza boasting of cordial relations as promised in the canto announcing the convoy's joyous arrival in Ohkay Owingeh but one that exposes Spanish ethnocentrism. Just as I have, his readers in 1610 might have realized that their laughter came at the expense of the indios, who were subjected to mean-spirited pranks and callous behavior. If his contemporaries laughed derisively, they laughed because they misread Villagrá's nuanced irony, an irony apparent to this reader four hundred years later.

Indeed, the more I reread Villagrá, the more it seems to me that he frames the middle section of the epic as a poetics of wonder and admiration for a native world the Spanish almost destroyed. When the poem turns to the kind of unrelenting warfare we remember from the *Iliad*, the stories of life on the llano cannot but establish aesthetic dissonance, as of two vastly opposing, seventeenth-century New World representations clashing before our eyes. The first is a world long settled and stable but without the insipidly romanticized language that permeates contemporary representations of Native Americans, a world at peace with itself, notwithstanding prolonged periods of scarcity, drought, and internecine warfare. The second is a world confused by lust for wealth and power in the far northern reach of empire—confused and disappointed by what it finds but no less arrogant and brutal. Before he is pulled into the vortex of slaughter the Spaniards brought on, Villagrá imagines an indigenous world imbued with profound knowledge for negotiating an ecology at once hard and fragile.

This indigenous architecture of survival is immediately apparent in Villagrá's record of the Plains people. Indeed, the poet seems most at ease and happiest when he is relating the stories of buffalo-hunting expeditions east of San Juan, out upon the plains that stretched over hundreds of miles and in which Europeans and Native people fill the narrative landscape of the middle cantos with a sense of new world possibility. These cantos of adventure—tales the men will tell their grandchildren years later—are, in Villagrá's hands, turned from callous boast to consideration of ruined possibility in the stories he tells of peaceful contact with Plains tribes, among the earliest in American literature, which resonate for contemporary readers with nuances similar to an entire sequence of narratives that trace the vast western American range.[31] Villagrá's description of the vast grasslands and innumerable buffalo is familiar to us all as a trope for a frontier ecology that has disappeared but that still carries the mythic power of a pre-colonial indigenous world where Plains people lived in cycles of balance, a time when hunting sustained a material and cultural world unknown to most Spaniards in the early seventeenth century. Villagrá's poem imaginatively relocates his Spanish audience upon a geography awesome in its grandeur, brimming with herds of animals that seemed a cross between the bulls of Spanish myth and those strange beasts of an even older mythic Greece:

todos juntos se metieron
Los llanos más adentro y encontraron
Tanta suma y grandeza de ganados
Que fue cosa espantosa imaginarlos.
Son de cuerpo que toros Castellanos,
Lanudos por extreme, corcobados,
De regalada carne y negros cuernos,
Lindíssima manteca y rico cebo,
Y como los chibatos, tienen barbas,
Y son a una mano tan ligeros
Que corren mucho más que los venados,
Y andan en atajos tanta suma
Que veynte y treynta mil cabezas juntas
Se hallan ordinarias muchas vezes.
Y gozan de unos llanos tan tendidos
Que por seyscientas y ochocientas leguas
Un sossegado mar parece todo,
Sin género de cerro ni vallado
Donde en manera alguna pueda el hombre
Topar la vista acaso o detenerla
En tanto quanto ocupa una naranja,
Si assí puede dezirse tal excesso. (17.81–102)

(Everyone together traveled / Further into the plains and found / Such great and mighty herds / That it was thing frightening to imagine them. / In shape they are like Spanish bulls, / Wooly in the extreme, humpbacked, / Of plentiful flesh and with black horns, / Most splendid lard and rich in fat, / And like he-goats, they have beards / And they are so swift afoot / That they run much faster than deer, / And move about in such great groups / That twenty and thirty thousand head / Are commonly found together. / And they enjoy such vast stretches of the llano / That for six-hundred and eight-hundred leagues / All seems like a quiet and calm sea / With neither valley nor hill / Where a man can / rest his vision or set it / Upon as much as the height of an orange, / And only so can its vastness be imagined [translation mine].)

Although Villagrá's is neither the first Spanish description of the buffalo nor of the llano, it is the first poetic description in American literature. The poet is filled with a sense of astonishment as he describes the beautiful, huge animals that once filled the sealike plains by the tens of thousands. Villagrá is writing beyond obligatory chronicle or verse memoir. After all, there were vivid descriptions of the buffalo in earlier Spanish *relaciones* that he appears to have used as source material, but that here he binds into storytelling. He must have read Pedro Castañeda's narrative of the Coronado expedition, which details some of the first European encounters with Plains people and the great buffalo herds and provided him much of the descriptive language he echoes in the *Historia*.[32] Indeed, because Villagrá was not actually present at the buffalo hunt he describes, we must assume that he was writing from accounts his friends provided him as well as from earlier reports he studied while composing his epic and that he artfully recombines in his own story.

The poet rolls earlier description into a verse narrative that peoples the llano with inhabitants from the colony, from various Pueblo and Plains tribes, as well as the Apache, all of whom are pictured hunting buffalo on the oceanlike grasslands. In the seventeenth canto, when the Spaniards try to corral part of the herd, the writer provides what has become a classic description of a mighty stampede: "La fuerza del ganado lebantando / Un terremoto espeso, tan cerrado / Que si junto a unas peñas no se halla / La soldadesca toda guarecida / No quedara ninguno que hecho piezas / Entre sus mismos pies no se quedara" (17.143–48) (When the herds raised an earthquake so thundering that had the soldiers not found protection by some nearby rocks they would all have been cut to pieces under their hooves). Earlier, a man named Marco Cortés kills a large deer that a group of Indian men are admiring. All at once, four women appear on the trail "With a large and well-loaded drove / Of dogs, which in these parts they use / To carry heavy burdens and work them / As though they were pack mules" (17. 41–44). Villagrá likens the dogs to Spanish mules and oxen, dragged down and injured from being carelessly overloaded. Cortés offers the deer to these women, they butcher and pack it off at once, and he rides deeper into the llano to hunt buffalo with his friends and the Apaches.

Villagrá's scenes about Spanish interaction with native people on the llano recall a joyous moment situated within an ethnographic matrix that offers his contemporary readers a sequence of stories about native dress, manners, expression, and distinct cultural practices. A Spanish reader would have seen cultural difference and yet noted similarities in certain everyday practices. Unlike the highly sentimental love tale the poet relates in canto thirteen of Polca and Milco—both fictional Indian characters who are nothing more than stock characters in a Spanish romance—the scenes he draws of the Plains Indians have a quality of verisimilitude, of close observation of native lifeways his audience in Spain would have read as accurate ethnographic record. Villagrá's sentiments here, however much narrowed by his own biases, disclose an unusually affirmative and yet dissonant sensibility within the century-long tradition of Spanish narratives about the llano, the buffalo, and the people who lived on this vast expanse. The result is that when one reads Cabeza de Vaca's *Relación* (c. 1542), the Coronado accounts of the 1540s, the Espejo report (1589), and then Villagrá's poem of 1610, all disclose Spanish regard for the indigenous and their culture at the same time the conquerors are marching over them. The poet too discloses his admiration for a people he and his fellow soldiers will, like Coronado's troopers sixty years earlier, soon destroy. Writing the poem ten years after his experience in la nueva México, Villagrá looks back with a sense of both wonder and regret, as when, in the same canto, he writes:

> Los quales vieron siempre en estos llanos
> Gran suma de vaqueros que apie matan
> Aquestas mismas vacas que dezimos
> Y dellas se sustentan y mantienen,
> Toda gente robusta y de trabajo,
> Desenfadada, suelta y alentada,
> Y tienen lindas tiendas por extremo
> Y lindos y luzidos pabellones
> Del cuero de las vacas, cuio adobo
> Es tan tratable y dozil que mojado
> Aqueste mismo cuero que dezimos
> Buelve después de seco más suabe
> Que si fuera de lienzo o fina olanda. (17.158–70)

(And we often saw upon these plains / A great many vaqueros [Apaches], who, traveling on foot, killed / These same buffalo I've described here / And from them they sustain and nourish themselves, / All a robust people and hard workers, / Joyful, free and courageous / And they live in very lovely tents / Very bright and pavilion-like, beautifully made / Of the buffalo hides, which are treated / To such a smooth and soft feel that when wet / That same leather we are describing / Becomes, when dry, / even softer / Than if it were of linen or fine Holland cloth [translation mine].)

As in his description of the Santo Domingo people, the poet honors the Apaches as "gente robusta y de trabajo," courageous, hunting the grasslands freely and joyfully, living in beautifully decorated buffalo-hide tents. His sentiments may seem disingenuous to contemporary postcolonial critics. I understand how a rhetoric of power superordinates one world view while it suppresses another, a language of admiration simply a ruse for glossing over the military denigration of native people. In Spanish colonial narrative, this rhetorical position usually takes the form of condescension, whether conscious of its aims or not. Yet there are two ways of thinking about Villagrá's literary reconstruction that keeps in tension opposing rhetorical aims. The first, as I have just stated, aims to restore a coherent indigenous world the Spanish were intent on destroying. The other emerges from what I think of as a kind of reverie produced by poetry itself, an imaginary of intellectual and emotive complexity, ideological self-conflict, an ambiguity of purpose that often startles Villagrá himself. This New World criollo is in contest with the imperial Spaniard he is. As he composes his *Historia*, the poem opens retrospectively to admiration for the people he had ten years earlier signed up to subdue. Villagrá's is an imperial imagination that traces its own ideological meanness in the decade after he left la nueva México, and yet, while in Spain, the center of gravity for the most expansive empire since Rome, the poet writes over and against empire as he tries to make sense of personal experience within the colonial enterprise.

In the very next canto, eighteen, we see just how confounding these warring sensibilities are for the criollo writer. This is the first time we hear from Zutacapán, the Acoma patriot, who presciently warns his people that the Spaniards intend to enslave them and insists they must preemptively resist or suffer the loss of their land and liberty. Zutacapán climbs to the top of a house and yells out to his people: "¿Será bien que perdamos todos juntos / La dulze libertad que nos dexaron / Nuestros difuntos padres ya passados? / ¿No sentís los clarines y las cajas / De la soberbia gente Castellana / Que a toda priessa viene ya marchando? / ¿Quál es aquél que piensa de vosotros / Quedar con libertad si aquéstos llegan" (Is it right that we altogether lose / The sweet freedom that was bestowed / By our ancestors now all gone? Do you not hear the trumpets and drums / Of those haughty Castilians / Who come marching in all haste? / Which one of you is there who thinks / To keep his liberty if they arrive?) (18.41–46). As we shall see in the following cantos, Zutacapán, a purely epic character Villagrá created, serves to justify Spanish brutality, yet he articulates the poet's recognition of native peoples' long knowledge of Spanish treachery.

Canto eighteen establishes the tension between two worlds that will end in another routine imperial show of force but not before the canto closes with the Spaniards and native people pictured as nearly hand-in-hand. Juan de Oñate, riding west with a small troop in search of silver deposits, escapes what appears to be a trap set for him on Acoma. At nearly the same moment, another Spanish group is greeted by a coalition of tribes in the surrounding area of the Zuni and Hopi nations, who in appeasement shower them with cornmeal, offer them food, and then invite them to participate in a hunt. The soldiers and some eight hundred Indians cooperate in a circle hunt, drawing "liebres, conejos y raposos" (18.355) (hare, rabbit and fox) into a tightening walking net. Villagrá renders the scene as a joyous moment. When some of the soldiers begin to dismount to hunt in unison with the Indians, they are expressly ordered to remain in their saddle, to remain on guard: "Por no saber de cierto si sus pechos / Fuessen tan buenos, nobles y cenzillos / Como ordinariamente se mostraron" (For not knowing for certain if their hearts / were as good, as noble and as pure / as they always show themselves to be) (18.364–66). The poet reveals his own inner heart here. The Spaniards do not dismount but do rein in their horses—these same horses that carried them across a perilous desert and are another machine of warfare—so that they can participate with the Zunis in a collective enterprise. The "joyous hunt" ("alegre caza") (18.367) is a huge success: a great many hares, rabbits, and foxes are gathered and shared in a feast about which Villagrá writes, "I do not know that the whole world has / Hares of a better taste, more savory / Larger, more beautiful or more tender / Than this land and neighboring country produce" (369–72). We witness a scene in which the poet imagines an alternate history. Trust and suspicion rub up against each other, and trust wins out against imperial power, at least for the moment. Villagrá recreates in 1610 the world he and other Spanish soldiers nearly destroyed in 1599, remembering it as bountiful, inhabited by people who had repeatedly proven themselves noble and pure of heart. A reader today—as well, perhaps, as one four centuries ago—wonders what might have happened had this compact been kept. Unfortunately for us all, Zutacapán's warning turns out to have been right.

In the middle cantos, then, rather than a paean to Juan de Oñate and the founding of la nueva México, Villagrá's *Historia* is largely an epic about Spain's confounded encounter with native America. In the cantos I have just discussed, consider how little Villagrá focuses on the day-to-day business of the settlers who, after a long journey, would have been establishing their stores, corralling the thousands of livestock they brought along, keeping their children from wading too far into the river, sewing and then washing clothes, repairing carts, closing doors to the cooling nights, and then waking to the sun, brilliant over the peaks of what they would come to call the Sangre de Cristo mountain range. In fact, there is nothing in the poem about everyday, common life in the colony, not a word about families, no stories of love affairs or feuds or scandals, although we know from the official historical records that many such incidents were recorded. On the contrary, a great many of the colonists who had braved the long, dry, and treacherous journey were so alienated within the first six months that they simply wandered away while Oñate was off on one or another of his explorations. They packed their belongings, their families, and their anger and simply returned to Mexico. Villagrá was among these disaffected colonists and his closing cantos, which chart the massacre at Acoma, serve as a reminder of the imperial policies that undid Spain's grand venture.

CHAPTER 3

Acoma:
El peñol ensangrado

~ 1 ~

One day not long ago, I visited the Sky City Cultural Center & Haakú Museum at Acoma and was amazed by an exhibition—*The Matriarchs*—that tells the story of four master potters whose loving designs recapture the pueblo's spiritual and aesthetic legacy. I looked closely at the hand-coiled clay jars there, which exemplify a history of how women pass down knowledge, belief systems, and cultural practice from mothers to daughters to granddaughters in this matrilineal society. On the official tour of the pueblo, the guide, a woman in her fifties, joked about the female duties: the women own the houses, maintain their care, and pass them down to the youngest daughter as a gift for watching the elders. The men, she explained, are farming off the mesa in the fields or in the kiva—the male domain—where they maintain the people's spiritual rituals, and, she teased, "where we send them to keep them from getting in the way." Her humor suggests a rich bond of understanding and cultural knowledge between genders that has remained steadfast over the centuries. There was no humor, however, when telling the pueblo's history. She spoke of the "cruelty of the Spanish" and then, as though having swatted off a fly, went on to tell us that we would have time to look at the "beautiful pots" people display on tables outside their doors. Lovely as they are to look at, these patterned jars insist that the near annihilation of the Acoma people in 1599 did not destroy their sense of belonging to the world around them or their profound loyalty to Haakú, the place that their deities had long before prepared for them.

The pots you can purchase if you go to the mesa today, like those preserved behind the Haakú Museum's glass, are richly embellished with designs that symbolize the people's relationship to the earth: thick rain clouds that nourish their crops, the hills and distant mountains that are sacred spots, the animals and cornstalks that provide them with sustenance. Parallel lines that run the length of the pots represent the rainfall the pueblo has waited for throughout the centuries and that they have built their lives around. Triangles signify mountains where the deities live and clouds form. The double-headed thunderbird, often depicted as an abstract curvilinear shape, represents both the complex cloud formations rising and filling the sky just before rain and the historical events passed down as story to children of visions the elders witnessed a long time ago. Deer, bighorn, and bear from Kaweshtima, the "woman mountain covered in snow," a peak that became Mount Taylor after the U.S.-Mexican War, provided food, hide material, and spiritual attributes fused into everyday life, and so they, too, are part of the stylish images on Acoma pottery.

Most of the designs for which the Acoma are famous emerge from figurations of the high-desert landscape of New Mexico. But one image emblazoned on their earthenware seems out of place in the land and sky here: the parrot. In an exhibit display case, nearly twenty jars, festooned with flowers or corn stocks, are set off by the bright reddish-feathered parrot perched on a branch whose curved bill is about to seize a cluster of berries and whose large, dark eye is alert and watchful. Curiously, this "Acoma parrot," as it has come to be called, is the most prominent symbol of the pueblo's pottery. Yet there have never been parrots or much in the way of berry trees in this part of the world.

The Haakú Museum guide, a young woman whose relatives are among the matriarchs, explained to me that "our ancestors sometimes brought back parrots" to the mesa. They did not survive long, she continued, because it was "too different here" for them. Nonnative anthropologists, on the other hand, have speculated that "there is abundant archaeological evidence that imported macaws and parrots were kept in the villages from at least AD 1100, possibly earlier, which indicates that their feathers were as important then as in modern ceremonies where they rank with those of eagles and turkeys."[1] An exhibit plaque mimics this assertion, claiming that "Mexican parrots were traditionally raised at Acoma for their beautiful feathers."[2] The young guide, poised in her matrilineal knowledge, smiled at this assertion and told me that while nobody remembers keeping parrots in the pueblo, people were often gone for long periods and brought back many items from the south, including bundles of bright red and orange feathers from parrots, macaws, and parakeets.

If we put archaeology and Pueblo oral history together, we get complementing rather than competing stories about the way cultural practice was disseminated over many centuries across Mexico and north into what the Spaniards called la nueva México. Tribal stories of trade are corroborated by anthropological research that suggests the Acoma, like most other native peoples, had traversed the wider pre-Columbian world. "At least from AD 1100, possibly earlier," archaeologists write, or, as the pueblo story goes, "Yeah, my grandma told me that this goes way back, way back." The parrot and macaw figures that find their way onto Acoma pottery tell us that the exchange of material culture, ideas, rituals and symbols, and news of major events circulated in ways that would have made manifest the arrival and depredations of the Spanish. In the years after 1520, when the great Aztec empire was leveled, and then again after Francisco de Coronado's devastating sweep across the Rio Grande corridor in the early 1540s, the troubling news Pueblo people brought home, bundled with trade items and brilliant feathers, would have been startling. In fact, the Acoma, who lived some sixty to seventy miles west of the Pueblos in the Rio Grande valley, would have known about Coronado's destructiveness there. People on the mesa must have hoped that the stories of ruin they had heard would remain distant. If not, they were prepared to defend their homes; after all, they had settled atop sheer sandstone walls four hundred feet above the desert floor as a defensive maneuver against others who had assailed them over the centuries. When you stand beneath the sheer vertical walls today, you can understand this people's sense of invulnerability. They climbed up the mesa cliff when nomadic tribes threatened to steal their hard-won harvests or when other Pueblo peoples, displaced by drought, considered moving in on them.[3] Peregrination and competition for natural resources led to tension and sometimes violence over the years, but these conflicts were family squabbles compared to their later encounter with the Spaniards.

The stories of Coronado's conquista must have produced long silences, anger, and troubled dreams, but then for sixty years the sun rose pink in the desert, and they waited as always for rain clouds to gather in the afternoon sky.[4] They continued farming the valley below. The corn, squash, and beans they harvested were stored on the mesa for the long winter months, and the water they needed for daily life was collected in cisterns wind-scooped out of the sandstone base of their lofty home. They were at peace with themselves and their neighbors until another group of Spanish intruders assaulted their patience and pride in 1599.

What befell the Acoma early that year might have destroyed a less determined people. Four centuries later, however, the pueblo is as sturdy a community as the rock upon which it sits. You can sense this determination in the architecture of the Haakú Museum itself, whose plunging verticals reproduce the mesa's sheer sandstone cliffs, or when, pulling open the heavy wood door, you enter what feels like sacred space, where tribal singing wafts through the halls. It is resolve I see in the faces of the young Acoma who greet visitors. Theirs is a resolve preserved over the centuries that, as former cultural center director Brian Vallo repeats in a video clip of the pueblo's history, will stand, people and pueblo, for another thousand years.[5]

~ 2 ~

I have been to Acoma many times as an adult, but where I grew up, we did not visit Indian pueblos. That was something only tourists—*los americanos*—did. For us it would have been an intrusion, or just strange. An uncle would have said, "What for, stupid?" In Albuquerque's South Valley, most of us were working-class Chicanos whose dads worked for the Santa Fe Railroad or at the base (Kirkland Air Force Base, that is), in the schools as custodians, or in the building trades. We knew better than to bother people at Isleta or Jémez or Acoma. When I took a class on the literature of the American Southwest at the University of New Mexico, though, my world began to admit greater complexity. The class opened with Paul Horgan's *Great River*, a classic history of the social and cultural formation of my own small geographical dot on the planet.[6] This course was really the beginning of my life as a literary historian, for after reading Horgan and a collection of novels, drama, and poetry about this land that was to become New Mexico, I was curious to understand more fully how literature traces historical formations and, conversely, how history is mirrored in poem and story. The class also provided my introduction to Native American and Chicano literature, which, I learned to my astonishment and wonder, had enjoyed a long history on the soil under my feet—though I must have been told just the opposite, because all I had read before was British literature and its offshoot, American literature of the eastern seaboard. The idea that literature had been produced over hundreds of years in the very spot where I was alive was a revelation and then something of a painful coming-to-consciousness about the social displacements so much of this narrative disclosed.

It was at this point, bashfully, that I visited Acoma. Prompted by our professor, a group of university friends and I drove the sixty miles to the pueblo on September 2 for the feast day of San Esteban, the patron saint of the Acoma, where we spent the afternoon in this remarkable village perched high above the desert floor. When you turn off Interstate 40 onto the small road that leads to Haakú, the land and sky open in an almost-perfect symmetry of blue expanse deepened by clouds spilling white spume, which later in the day darken toward rain. Open to the eye in every direction, the land is etched with juniper, rabbit bush, sage, and clump grasses against backdrops of sandstone cliffs and sheer walls that rise into heaven. When you arrive at the mesa that has been home to the Acoma for more than a thousand years, your sight fixes upon a conjunction of stone, two-storied pueblo homes and an immensity of sky that gladdens. What I remember always about Acoma is this surrounding capaciousness, the eye's surprise at seeing so far across the circling horizon, and then, closer at hand, the clustered homes, the voices sharp in the thin air, ricocheting from around corners, the barking of dogs, the sharp falling angles and upward gliding of ravens calling in their own cawing barks. When you approach the edge of the cliff your heart momentarily feints at an imagined falling, a swoosh of sky, or, if you have flying dreams, you ease off the ledge and float over the mesa, lifting higher until land become a single sheet of flatness beneath you.

On a feast day at Acoma all of the rough edges of social disruption smooth away. Every September 2, the residents open their pueblo to all. The day begins with mass in the church of San Esteban, after which the people take the bulto (carved wood statue) of the saint and set it in a shrine where it will remain through the day, with the war chiefs guarding it while people dance in tight lines until evening, when these same chiefs are touched gently with cornmeal by the dancers. Legend has it, the Acoma guide will say when you visit now, that in 1629, when fray Juan Ramírez was making his way up the mesa, one of the women watching in an angry crowd dropped her daughter in the commotion. Fray Ramírez caught the child or retrieved her from the floor of the mesa—there are still variants of the story—but in either case, the event was regarded as miraculous. The pueblo allowed Ramírez to climb the stairwell where, by helping rebuild the pueblo, he gained their trust. When he had won them over to Roman Catholicism, they erected the enormous church of San Esteban, with its massive timber vigas set on seventy-foot walls to lift the nave high in the heavens.[7] Today the Acoma people graciously invite visitors to church and pueblo for this special feast day. They are unguarded in their generosity, inviting people into their homes for posole, horno-baked bread, and red and green chile, always welcoming and gracious.

Not so fast—history disrupts legend, and memory refuses easy reconciliation. If the Acoma people trusted one Franciscan priest, they would never again trust the Spanish, nor would they forget the devastation that took place in 1599. Some thirty years after the Spaniards had all but destroyed the pueblo, killed or punished with servitude and dispersal hundreds of its people, the Acoma slowly rebuilt not only their village but also the culture of daily life—and this against continued impositions. "The cruelty of the Spanish," the phrase I remember hearing from the pueblo tour guide on my first visit and on every visit since over the years, marks this story. Most recently the guide recalled how "those Spanish who were welcomed to the pueblo" (in December 1598) started "demanding things." When a soldier stole one woman's turkeys, the guide said, there was a skirmish that ended in the death of thirteen Spaniards. A month later, a group of seventy soldiers dressed in battle gear returned and destroyed everything in three days. "Many of our ancestors were killed," she told us, "and five hundred were captured and punished."

If, like me, you grew up Chicano in New Mexico, the dislocations your own people continue to endure in the present often blur a sobering connection to a destructive colonial history. Too often we forget our complicity in displacing native people over the history of our brief four centuries in this land. We celebrate a long presence in Nuevo México, many times overlooking, forgetting, and ignoring the destruction our ancestors participated in, claiming, in a convenience of cultural mestizaje, a connection with indigenous origins insufficient to describe the reality of Nuevomexicano history. I am not arguing here for that insipid fiction of direct Spanish descent with which the colonial preservationists lullaby themselves. Yet, Nuevomexicanos roundly and repeatedly participate in festivals of culture that dramatize a genealogy predicated on Spanish colonial continuity that makes a fairy tale of military domination: festivals such as Juan de Oñate's yearly entrada at the Española fiesta; the ritual performances of *Moros y Cristianos* or *Los Comanches* dramatized in towns and villages; the processional opening of the Santa Fe Fiesta that commemorates don Diego de Vargas's peaceful reoccupation of the City of Holy Faith in 1692, which was, in fact, a military reoccupation after the Pueblo Revolt of 1680.

The difficulty here is to negotiate continuity and contradiction. How, that is, can we affirm a long and sustaining cultural presence and yet speak the truth about Spanish colonial violence? Where there is a history of intercultural friendship and blood mixture, there is also a legacy of violence and cultural arrogance. We know that Gaspar Pérez de Villagrá participated in the slaughter and humiliation of the Acoma only to give voice, however imaginary, to these same people, raising them to heroic stature while simultaneously demonizing them, recreating and celebrating the Spanish victory while exposing a Spanish policy of annihilation and imperial mendacity.

If *Historia de la Nueva Mexico* is, as Manuel Martín-Rodríguez argues, a hybrid text that deliberately fluctuates between literary discourse and historiography, I would likewise say that the fluctuation between history and the literary in the first two major sections of the poem gives way almost entirely to epic in the final cantos that dramatize the battle at Acoma.[8] It is precisely at this point that the *Historia* turns toward a poetry of historical fabulation more akin to Virgil's *Aeneid* than to an eyewitness account. Or, if an eyewitness account, the poem is one whose epic sensibility eludes the force of official document. Villagrá's turn to epic has been regarded as a cunning strategy to occlude what really took place at Acoma on January 21–24, 1599, by deflecting attention to a stylized Virgilian drama that preempts charges of the war crimes about to be leveled at Oñate and his officers—the writer included.

Indeed, José Rabasa offers just such a reading of the poem's rhetorical logic when he writes: "Villagrá seeks to vindicate Oñate and all those who participated in the massacre at Acoma."[9] On a first reading, Villagrá's literary maneuver in the prolonged battle scene may leave one with the impression that he substitutes Virgilian epic for a historical chronicle of the lopsided victory in order to "legitimize the war against Acoma." "Ideological validation of the massacre," as Rabasa argues, would be more fully achieved through epic drama that glosses over the terror imposed upon the Acoma, making this destruction palatable for an audience familiar with epic structure. Yet after reading the final cantos through again and again, I am convinced it is precisely by turning to the classical model that Villagrá renders the massacre at Acoma an act of senseless cruelty. By prolonging the graphic landscape of death in these last verses, Rabasa insists, Villagrá's description produces not revulsion but aesthetic pleasure for a seventeenth-century audience presumably unsympathetic to the plight of indigenous Americans.[10] This just does not square with either the content of the poem or the colonists' allegations against Oñate. Had the poem been used in the criminal proceedings against Oñate and his lieutenants—and there is no record it was—it undoubtedly would have provided ironclad evidence of the brutality for which, through other testimony Oñate's settlers offered, the general and his principals were found guilty.

For contemporary readers, the poem rips apart any romance of the first Spanish colonial settlement. Anyone who has visited Acoma and has read historical accounts of what took place in January 1599 cannot but be heartsick when reading Villagrá's account of the battle. A reader is confronted by stark images of violence: people hacked to pieces, eviscerated, decapitated, mounds of bodies. So, although I bring a contemporary sensibility to my own reading of the poem—insisting as I do that one should visit Acoma and the country surrounding it to fully understand the poem's symbolic power in rendering the massacre—I believe that Villagrá intended to produce a literary text that would expose a dominant military machine's butchery of the Acoma. Had Villagrá wanted to draw attention away from Spanish savagery, he might well have written a few battle cantos and then gone back to describe the colonial project. Had he wished to avoid culpability, he might easily have glossed over the three-day battle as Oñate and other Spaniards did in their reports, narrating instead the colonizing events that would bring his *Historia de la Nueva Mexico* to closure. Just a month after the battle, Oñate casually mentions the incident in his own report to the Viceroy (March 2, 1599)—"I razed and burned their pueblo." He goes on to describe the "pearl bearing shells of unusual size" and "the great wealth that the mineral lodes have begun to reveal" in his frenetic explorations—all of which, as I have noted in earlier chapters, were contrived.[11] Mimicking Oñate's evasive history, Villagrá might have dramatized the embryonic formation of an agricultural colony, with attention to the heroism of everyday life by a group of people marooned in a strange land. He might have closed his poem in 1610 by noting that three years before Oñate was called to Mexico to answer charges, the governor moved the Spanish settlement to what would become Santa Fe. Inaugurating its capital would have been more befitting a poem titled *Historia de la Nueva Mexico*. Villagrá instead turned to the unremitting representation of warfare, the *Iliad* and *Aeneid* providing him a language of bloody saturation in which violence unrelentingly reminds readers of the brutal stupidity of the Spanish victory at Acoma.

Villagrá, I think, was transfixed by the massacre at Acoma. This violent event became the nightmare history fixed forever in a poem that links itself to a chain of Old and New World epics offering sustained meditation on the savage brutality, political arrogance, and masculine stupidity of war. The classical literature and history Villagrá read as a student at the Universidad de Salamanca in the 1570s not only provided an epic structure for the *Historia* but also established for the nascent poet the emotional locus for his reflections on war, abstracted perhaps by the dramatic language of epic, but not so far distanced as to be transformed into historical monument or myth, as was the case for Homer and Virgil. For Villagrá, by contrast, the literary reenactment of warfare could never merely be an aesthetic gloss premised on the fortunate coincidence of his participation in the siege of Acoma that found a corollary in the last six cantos of the *Aeneid*, the New World adventurer celebrating his exploits in the Roman style. Rather, it seems to me, the gruesome depictions of brutality he remembered from the *Iliad* and the *Aeneid* must have startled Villagrá, making him recall all at once the grim reality of the slaughter at Acoma: sword gashes in flesh, blood spurting from severed limbs, bodies eviscerated by cannon shot, skulls split, brains dashed, faces broken apart. He was haunted, I believe, by the mounds of bodies he and his Spanish compatriots had left heaped on a cliff mesa ten years before.

Did Virgil's text of war allow Villagrá to sublimate Spanish violence? It probably did, up to a point. After all, one imagines that epic, with its unremitting images of man-to-man battle, provided Villagrá with a model for representing violence that might allow a provident distance from Acoma. Though his contemporary readers might well have heard echoes of the *Aeneid* (especially books six through twelve), they could not be gulled into overlooking the unfolding violence in this far northern province by setting Virgil and Villagrá side-by-side as purely literary. On the contrary, Oñate's carnival trial of the Acoma survivors "made news throughout New Spain and in Europe for many years."[12] Though after the trial Oñate wanted to get on with the business of finding what he had come for, the nightmare violence doomed another Spanish expedition to chimera.

As Villagra's audience read the Virgilian reenactment of war against the Acoma, the *Aeneid* would become its palimpsest, or shadow text, just as Virgil's Roman readers, steeped in Greek poetry and drama, would have discerned echoes of recent events and the troubled state of contemporary political affairs through the sheen of an epic history that had long receded into the domain of myth.[13] Indeed, Virgil was intent on producing a literary work that would at once summon Homer while simultaneously engaging in an exaltation and critique of Rome in its last fifty years before Christ's birth. Remember: Felipe III was Villagrá's ideal first reader, just as Caesar Augustus was Virgil's. The King, Villagrá must have known, would glimpse himself and Spain in Virgil's foundation epic while being reminded of the violence his own empire had wrought upon the New World. If Virgil's motive for writing the *Aeneid* was in part to encourage Augustus to turn away from war so that he might repair the state, perhaps Villagrá wished to compare the destruction of Acoma with that of Troy to encourage the crown and Spain to understand the curse such military waste brought about. After all, Oñate was brought to trial in 1614 and found guilty of brutality at Acoma.

Though *Historia de la Nueva Mexico* has been thought to celebrate empire and rationalize colonial dominion, it unavoidably and forcefully reenacts the devastating effect of imperial violence. As far as I know, neither prosecution nor defense used Villagrá's poem at the trial. Had it been used, it seems to me that the Acoma section laid out the Spanish destruction of the pueblo so forcefully that the no heroic gloss of verse could have hidden a massacre. In his poem, I read contradictory self-disclosure, ideological ambiguity, and guarded compassion in a nightmare epic composed by a criollo soldier who had participated in the destruction of 1599 and was also ordered to stand trial. Memory fills the classical images he borrowed from Virgil with reminders of a loathsome violence against people whose lifeways Villagrá has just affirmed in the preceding cantos. For Villagrá, the stark battle scenes offer a personal space for representing culpability. Culpa: a sin confessed obliquely in epic verse; *Historia de la Nueva Mexico*: a book of carnage for the world to read.

Lust of steel
Raged in him, brute insanity of war,
And wrath above all . . .
So, then, in violation of the peace,

> He told the captains of his troop to march
> ordering arms prepared,
> The land defended, and the enemy
> Pushed back from the frontiers ...
> His orders given, vows made to the gods,
> His countrymen cheered one another on,
> And vied with one another to make war. (7.635–54)

Anger, "lust of steel," and the "brute insanity" that engenders war characterize this defiant speech. Yet, land and home must be defended and the enemy pushed back to the frontiers. For the Acoma, as for native people throughout the Americas, such defiance led to near annihilation, followed by a "peace" in which they suffered the imposition of vassalage, the unwarranted but iron expectation that they submit to the exploitation of their land and labor. One of Juan de Oñate's first actions in October 1598 was to assemble the Acoma tribal leaders and impose the "Act of Obedience and Homage," a public acknowledgement of their obedience to the king of Spain.[14] Pueblos up and down the river valley had already made their pledge; now the Acoma would make theirs. They retreated to their fortress, but many Acoma seethed and turned a slanting look, unyielding, against these invaders who "must be pushed from the frontiers."

Wait—this is Virgil's Turnus speaking Latin rage and defiance against the Trojans, not Villagrá's Zutacapán shouting from the mesa cliff. Here, the two men—literary characters and ideological figures—are cousins in their rage against invasion and humiliating homage. Zutacapán's equal wrath is reminiscent of the angry sentiments we hear from Prince Turnus and other Latin citizens when Aeneas shows up on "Lavinium shores and Italian soil" (1.3) expecting everyone to embrace a new regime prophesied by the gods. Villagrá begins the *Historia* by gesturing to Virgil when he refers to Oñate as Aeneas (although, as I have already suggested, Oñate proves too disappointing a historical figure for Villagrá to mythify) and must have had his copy of Virgil close at hand when writing the last, long account of the Spanish destruction of Acoma. Ercilla's *La Araucana* provided Villagrá with a companion New World text with which to imagine the imperial soldier as a dog of war, but Virgil's epic provided the Spanish poet with his primary model. Villagrá does not casually ransack the *Aeneid* or *La Araucana* for shocking images of war, nor will his troubled memory summarily permit an aesthetic deflection from the reality of an unjust war against the Acoma. Rather these earlier epics provide Villagrá with a formal literary structure for thinking about colonial power in the Americas.

When he returned to Spain and drafted a literary chronicle of his experience on the far northern frontier, the vogue for New World epic motivated Villagrá to try his hand at writing a verse account of his exploits, but recollection of a near genocide flashed within him, spiraling inward with the force of a vortex, pulling the writer toward nightmare images of eviscerated bodies piled in a tangle and the ruined, smoking village he and his comrades had left behind. Villagrá must have been hard pressed to push away this memory of the massacre, a vision of death that could not but define it as the overwhelming reality of his participation in the expedition. The massacre gathered finally and fully in the last crescendoing movement of the poem. Here readers discover a sharp turn toward the fictive, where historical chronicle takes on a dramatic structure. The landscapes Homer and Virgil evoke find a corollary in Villagrá's geography of desert valleys and mesas—one mesa in particular reminiscent of walled Troy or Numantia, the doomed Iberian fortress. In earlier cantos, characters can be identified as actual members of the expedition, but in its final movement the poem takes on the quality of tragedy, its people speaking ideas and emotions with an immediacy the first two-thirds of the poem does not offer readers. Villagrá fashions native characters whose words frame sharp rejoinders to the Spanish invaders, and we read epic oratory, debate amongst principals, heroic speeches launching assaults, furious battle cries, and anguished words spoken over the bodies of fallen comrades. The fury that Prince Turnus displays against the Trojan invaders in the *Aeneid* shaped Villagrá's recollection of Acoma's fierce resistance, and it was that resistance that infused epic mimicry with visceral truth.

Villagrá's speeches, Bruce R. Smith derisively argues, "have been filtered through the established models from European historiography and literature."[15] This is hardly strange, however. Steeped in a European literary tradition, it is not surprising—though it seems to be to Smith—that Villagrá would structure his own characters in a form consistent with earlier models, down to the words that came out of their mouths. Turnus, not to mention numerous other epic characters, provides Villagrá with a New World figure of resistance in Zutacapán, the primary voice of Acoma's distrust:

"Escuchadme varones y mujeres,
Vecinos desta fuerza desdichada,
Que a dura servidumbre miserable

> Hos siento ya sugetos y abatidos,
> ¿Por quál razón abéys assí querido
> Dormir a sueño suelto sin cuidado?
> ¿Será bien que perdamos todos juntos
> La dulze libertad que nos dexaron
> Nuestros difuntos padres ya passados?
> ¿No sentís los clarines y las cajas
> De la soberbia gente Castellana
> Que a toda priessa viene ya marchando?
> ¿Quál es aquél que piensa de vosotros
> Quedar con libertad si aquéstos llegan,
> Estando como estamos descuidados?
> Tomad, tomad, las armas y esperemos
> La intención, mala o buena, con que vienen,
> Que en nuestra mano está después dejarlas
> Si conviene, assí, que las dexemos." (18.34–53)

(Listen to me, honorable men and women / Neighbors in this unhappy place / That to a hard and miserable servitude / I fear we are now doomed and fated. / Is it good that we all together lose / That sweet freedom that was left to us / By those, our ancestors, who came before us? / Do you not hear the trumpets and drums / Of those haughty Castilians / Who at great speed march upon us? / Which of you amongst us thinks that we / Will keep our freedom if they arrive / Being, as we are, all careless? / Take, take up arms and let us await prepared / The intentions, evil or worthy, with which they come. / For it is in our hands to lay them down / If it shall seem best to lay them down [translation mine].)

So says Zutacapán. He climbs to the top of one of the pueblo houses and declares that Acoma is in grave danger and must prepare for an inevitable assault by the Spaniards. Villagrá, obviously, would have numbered himself among the "haughty Castilians," and yet he makes himself the scribe for indigenous resistance in language that borrows from nationalist phrasing. Villagrá incongruously gives equal footing here to native will to autonomy, notwithstanding the course of empire that, as his earlier inclusion of the act of possession makes clear, breaches and breaks all indigenous sociopolitical structures. Moments later, when Zutacapán's words have had the desired effect of rousing the pueblo to arms, with people taking up their war maces, shields, and bows, Zutacapán issues the battle cry that Spanish readers would have recognized as purely their own: "Guerra, Guerra / A sangre, fuego y arma, sin remedio / Ni dilación"

(18.73–74) (War, War / By blood, fire, and arms, without hesitation, / nor delay). In this section, Villagrá is, it seems to me, consciously manipulating received literary form and nationalist rhetoric in a manner that throws the Spanish rationale for the massacre into doubt.

To this day in New Mexico, the reason the Hispanic cultural preservationists give for the Spanish destruction of Acoma is as recompense for the deaths of thirteen men who had scaled the fortress in late December of 1598. When in canto twenty-two a group of soldiers is attacked on the mesa for, as the Acoma guides remember today, "demanding things," we hear Zutacapán shout: "Death! Death by blood and fire! Death / To all these thieves" (22.123). Villagrá resituates the well-known Spanish clarion call of empire and by placing it in Zutacapán's mouth ironizes the colonial rhetoric that rationalizes massacre. In a similar radical displacement, another warrior shouts, "Mueran estos fementidos, / Infames, viles, perros alebosos, / Perturbadores del común sossiego!" ("Death to the false and unfaithful, / Infamous, vile, and treacherous dogs, / Disturbers of our common peace") (22.132–34). We know in hindsight that this fictional character's warning was well founded, but Villagrá still writes dialogue in which Acoma's leaders, like the figures in Greek and Roman epic, debate opposing responses to the intrusion. Zutacapán takes "the chief hand / In defending the fatherland" in refusing to allow these "foreigners and strange people . . . to set foot inside their fort" (20.333–46).

At first glance it appears odd or self-serving that Villagrá would style Acoma speech as debate, since of course he could not possibly have heard their exchanges or even known that they likely met in kiva council to determine a course of action. Like Virgil, though, he uses classical rhetoric to stage imperial politics, defiance against power, and loyalty to community over and against greed for power. Certainly Zutacapán, who is described as having little standing in the "grave councils" of the tribe and is "eager . . . to be considered great" (21.16–17), allows Villagrá to establish a rationale for overthrowing the pueblo, portraying this leader of the resistance as "Luzbel" (21.16) (Lucifer), a man of "cruel, unmeasured haughtiness" (cruel soberbia, desmedida) (21.21), always "burning and glowing" with anger (21.24). Yet, modeled as he is on Virgil's Turnus, this figure represents a nationalist ideal that must have created a kind of double recognition in Villagrá's contemporary readers. Surely they would have recognized that native peoples remained intimidated by, but also defiant of, Spanish domination nearly a century after Cortés conquered Tenochtitlán. Bartolomé de las Casas's *Brevísima relación de la destrucción de las Indias* (1552) and the Leyes Nuevas of 1542–52 would not let them forget. By refiguring Las Casas's representations of cruelty to native people, Villagrá, like Ercilla twenty years earlier, would remind them, obliquely, perhaps, but not unwittingly.

The Spanish would also always remember their centuries-long defiance of the Moorish invasion. Granted, the intoxications of empire might have blinded them to their own history of subordination, but I believe the residual recollection of resistance to the Moorish conquest of Spain might well have prompted recognition and admiration of native defiance in Villagrá's readers. This admiration surfaces in Ercilla's *La Araucana*, that other New World tribute to the near destruction of native Chilean people. Villagrá, we know, read Ercilla, but whereas Ercilla's book is an appropriately titled tribute to Araucanian resistance to the Spaniards, we see in Villagrá a kind of ambiguity or tension in the narrative made recognizable by the literary prefigurations of classical and New World epic. Villagrá would have seen empire through Virgil's literary sensibility rather than Ercilla's poetics, since like Virgil, who wrote as one of the emperor's favorites, Villagrá composed in the midst of the Spanish court. Like the Roman, too, Villagrá subtly dramatized the empire's unwarranted meanness against local people through native characters whose rage uncompromisingly expresses their affront. Zutacapán argues for deceiving the Spaniards in a "trato doble" (21.210) for, after all, the intruders have done nothing but lie, steal, and brutalize the neighboring pueblos. No doubt the King's audience would have heard the echoes of Zutacapán's censure of Spanish presumption and arrogance. Such rhetorical structures—in Virgil and in Villagrá—evoke competing ideological positions, offering representations at once loyal to and complicit with empire and yet surging with unresolved anxiety about one's place in the colonial death machine. Ever since Las Casas made his case against the wholesale violence visited upon native people, there was gathering support in Spain for greater oversight of the colonies. The laws issued in 1542 and then revised and weakened in 1552 enacted a series of measures meant to protect the Indians from labor exploitation, excesses, or ill treatment. Of course, violence against Indians did not stop with the King's decrees, but increasingly there were attempts to bring to justice those colonists who transgressed the laws. Oñate's trial and conviction in 1614 is an instance of such juridical application.

Consider the complexity of positioning Villagrá negotiates as Zutacapán speaks his anger in the face of Spanish trepidation: "Say what more infamous and vile affront / Can come upon all of this fortress (aquesta fuerza) / Than to permit so harsh a servitude (dura servidumbre) / As giving food to strangers, / We all being free as they? (¿Siendo, como ellos, todos libertados?) (21.33–37). Elsewhere, the narrator describes Zutacapán as "un astuto lobo / Por la nariz y boca resollando" (a cunning wolf snorting aloud through nose and mouth). Here, though, Zutacapán's response to Spain's exploitative habit of appropriating corn, fowl, blankets, and other supplies from Acoma—not to mention nearly all the pueblos they encountered in their march—is perfectly reasonable. He is more audacious in arguing that the native people are as free as the Spanish invaders—those demanding, arrogant leeches who, stupid to native culture and social organization, regarded the stable and self-sufficient pueblos as "bárbaros." Wouldn't his first reader, the King, have been called to account when reading a fictional "bárbaro" refer to "la dulze libertad que nos dexaron / Nuestros difuntos padres ya passados" (That sweet liberty that was left / By those, our ancestors, who came before us)? Villagrá's contradictory inscription recalls the double vision Virgil structured into the *Aeneid* when he celebrated Augustus's imperial Rome, yet offered a stinging critique of Rome's savage militarism through the speeches of the poem's Latin characters. As R. D. Williams argues, Virgil's public voice is an affirmation of Augustan Rome, but there is also a "private" Virgil whose literary sensibilities offer a more sobering reflection on a Rome steeped in petty politics, self-serving policy making, and rapacious violence.[16] Villagrá's complex representations of the pueblo's will to autonomy convince me that he recognized this private Virgil and, against his own recorded affirmation of the expedition, turned to the *Aeneid* as a way of thinking through the moral cost of empire. It is indeed through mimesis of Greek and Roman oratorical structure and the savage spectacle of warfare that the *Historia* registers Villagrá's private doubt, self-contempt, and, I think, grief.

The debate in the *Historia* may seem contrived until one realizes that Villagrá is thinking through the conflicting dimensions of an event that, given what we know from its historical versions, might have been avoided. Just as the eleventh book of the *Aeneid* dramatizes the debates between Turnus and more conservative Latin elders, Villagrá's eighteenth canto stages the argument between Zutacapán and the tribal elder, Chumpo, over the death that his defiance has caused. In Virgil, after a pitched battle has "heaped up in mammoth carnage, bodies jumbled, / numberless and nameless. Everywhere," Drances, a council elder, denounces Turnus for his "bluster" and "baleful influence" that "put out so many of our shining lights ... that we see our city founder in grief." Zutacapán, likewise, articulates a militaristic position that other tribal members opposed. While this argument is obviously constructed through a European literary and imperial discourse, it considers what might have happened if Juan Zaldívar and his men had not "demanded things" and if, having been confronted by Spanish arrogance, the Acoma had resisted the justifiable but doomed response Zutacapán exacts. Knowing full well how Spanish rapaciousness devastated any show of resistance through "sangre y fuego"—total warfare—the warning to remain vigilant but peaceful that Zutacapán's son Zutancalpo and the pueblo elder, Chumpo, argued for suggests that native people commonly met in council to reason through tribal responses to external threats. The rhetorical exchanges in epic speech allow Villagrá to think about what happened in late 1598 in ways that voice arrogance shaded by regret, an affirmation of empire unsettled by soul-killing violence, the recognition of religious beneficence over and against a history of Christian intolerance and cruelty.

Of course, Villagrá may be said to exploit epic speech merely to rationalize the Spanish assault. Perhaps by putting incriminating words into the mouths of the Acoma he offered preemptive defense against charges of military cruelty, as Smith and José Rabasa suggest. Yet Villagrá structured debate following the classical model so as to present alternate ideologies, competing social philosophies, and, though it may appear self-serving, to give voice to indigenous responses to the Spanish military threat. If only Zutacapán had not roused his people to a war that had to lead to their massacre—that is, if only the Acoma had acquiesced to their subordination, they would not have suffered such violence. If only, Villagrá might have mused, the Acoma had kept their poise rather than thrown "the vile, and treacherous dogs" off their mesa home. All wishful history, ultimately, since Villagrá is ideologically complicit with Spanish mendacity. Nonetheless, Zutacapán provides Villagrá a rhetorical space through which, like Bernal del Castillo a century before him, he remembers his own role as a soldier, a man of flesh and blood who in January 1599 threw a wooden beam across a rock cliff and partook in the killing of hundreds of Acoma people. A decade later he published a poem whose sweep of twelve thousand lines broodingly meditates on the physical and spiritual turmoil war exacts from its soldiers.

When it comes to his sense of history, my cousin Eddie is like a lot of Chicanos in New Mexico: he "kind of knew that our people had done some bad shit back then." One evening we sat outside in Placitas drinking beer as we looked toward the Santa Ana Pueblo mesa. When I explained what had taken place at Acoma in 1599, he peered outward, his cigarette drawing into an ash tail as he listened. When I told him why the first group of Spaniards had been killed in December, he just gave one of those Chicano nods as if to say, "Yeah, that don't surprise me." When I explained that seventy soldiers were sent back to Acoma to punish the tribe, he asked, "Only seventy guys? Weren't there a lot more indios?" "Sure," I said, "but the Spanish had guns and steel swords and cannons." "Yeah, that's right," he nodded again. When I described how the Spanish killed hundreds of Acoma, dispersed the survivors, put them into servitude, and then cut a foot off every man older than twenty-five, he gave voice to an expression less measured: "They did what? Shhh, our ancestors were mean, *ese*."

Now you have to understand: Eddie is a working guy. He has had a tough life, done stuff he shouldn't have in a tough neighborhood, been in trouble with the law at times. He went to Vietnam as a kid of seventeen and grew up in a flash of gunfire and napalm. Like other men who have seen killing and done killing, he is tight-lipped about battle. For him there is nothing to celebrate or joke about—and there is no forgetting. Between draughts on a cold beer and draws on a smoke, he would only say, "I seen things you wouldn't believe, man." When I read him sections from Villagrá describing the carnage at Acoma and then commented that the Spaniards had done things I could not believe, he just looked at me as if I were too stupid to understand such hardness and said, "That's war, *ese*. You do what's ordered. Guys get torn up." He was not making excuses for the Spanish, but, it seemed to me, saying what a soldier would say about war, whether a conflict that ended thousands of years in the past, his war in Vietnam, or the butcherings taking place somewhere right now. We can critique "empire" all we want from the comfort of our university offices, but it was people like Eddie and that other soldier, Gaspar Pérez de Villagrá, who fired the guns. Villagrá and his companions carried out the massacre at Acoma as part of an imperial killing machine, but they were not themselves machines, however unfeeling we assume them to have been under their suits of steel. Looking away, Eddie told me that he woke up every day remembering what he had done. After nightmares of broken bodies, a carnival of killing, he had to decide each morning if he would face the world or kill himself. What I, sitting at my desk, can only guess at by reading.

More than any book I have read, it was Eddie who taught me in that wrenching conversation that soldiers carry the violence of battle with them throughout their lives. Men who have killed people in war, he told me with words, eyes, and a clenched physicality, do not forget. Nor, usually, do they gloat. Villagrá wrote an epic to memorialize empire, and yet, as we shall see, his verse does not revel in the blood-gush of images. Like Eddie, he is self-effacing—hardly present in his own narrative and yet everywhere narrating war. When called to duty, he carried out his orders and then slighted himself as unimportant, whether as a reconnaissance scout or when he threw a log across a chasm atop Acoma to save his fellow soldiers during the onset of battle. Perhaps this is false humility, as some of his readers believe. The violence that burdens memory, though—his own experience in war conflated with the archetypal landscapes of Homer and Virgil—produces an estranging juxtaposition between Villagrá the soldier and Villagrá the poet.

Since we know relatively little about the man, we must turn again to the poem. Here, literary tradition and epic topoi open a figurative space in which the poet confronts what needs to be suppressed in the everyday, the remembered violence that has remained coiled inside years after he left la nueva México. As he sets pen to paper, what Villagrá remembers about the events of January 1598 seeps and then gushes out in a drama that provides both aesthetic distance and dissociative plentitude. That is, as rendered in the poem, the battle of Acoma is a gruesome fiction, a series of nightmare images distilled from epic rather than purely from chronicle; here, fiction and chronicle collide with such force that what took place in 1598–99 can never be put aside as the minor skirmish Juan de Oñate noted in his letter to the Viceroy in 1599.

The scene in which Juan de Zaldívar and twelve other Spanish soldiers are killed on the mesa top recalls the treacheries inscribed in classical literature that were premised on remote events, but the historical event Villagrá dramatizes in epic form was recorded in the "Trial of the

CHAPTER 3

Indians of Acoma, 1598," a patently one-sided account that mostly suppresses what occurred.[17] In early December, Zaldívar, the *maese de campo*, rode west to join Oñate, along with some thirty men. When the group arrived at Acoma, the trial proceeding reads, Zaldívar "asked the Indians for provisions for this trip and gave in exchange hatchets and many other things." In reply, "the Indians very unwillingly gave some maize and tortillas."[18] The account goes on to indicate that the maese reminded them that they had "unanimously sworn obedience to this majesty" and that what the soldiers "needed most was flour."[19] It is then, the trial chronicles, that Zaldívar and his men were attacked with "premeditation and treachery." He and twelve others were killed, while another five men jumped from the four-hundred-foot cliff, four of them somehow surviving to give account in the proceedings. Their testimonies are brief and of nearly a single voice: the Spaniards ask for provisions in a friendly manner, the Acoma reluctantly offer a few tortillas, Zaldívar orders his men not to cause "the Indians any harm" (446), the Acoma split the men up and attack them without provocation.[20] Juan Blázquez de Cabanillas's account of the skirmish can stand for them all:

> This witness, Captain Diego Núñez, and other soldiers went to a few houses where some gave a little, but others pulled up their ladders and refused to give up any. Meanwhile this witness saw that one of the many Indians who followed us uttered a loud cry and then all began to do likewise and both men and women attacked from the terraces and from the ground with many arrows, stones, and other missiles, and pressed us so hard that Hernando de Segura was soon felled by a stone; many others, wounded and covered with blood and half dead, sought protection among the rocks nearby.... This witness jumped from the rock and reached the horses, although badly bruised. After this he was able to help some of the wounded men who had jumped from the rocks, one of them being Juan de León, who was badly wounded and could not stand up.... By now he noticed that the Indians in the pueblo mockingly wore the hats and brandished the swords of the dead.[21]

Villagrá's epic rendering deepens and complicates the testimonials. In Cabanillas's testimony a nameless Indian "uttered the loud cry"; in the poem, however, it is Zutacapán whose "cry raised a bold uproar / Of the infernal, warlike mob" (infernal canalla belicosa) (22.135–36). Whereas Cabanillas testifies, as do the other survivors, that "both men and women attacked from the terraces and from the ground with many arrows, stones, and other missiles," Villagrá gives fictional names to the individual Acoma and locates the battle more clearly in time and space. One man, Bibero, he writes, is killed when "a mighty rock / Was by a weak old woman thrust. / This fell straight down in such a way / As smashed his head into pieces / His hidden brains now scattered wide" while "Popolco did attack one Costilla, / A mulatto by race ... / And, slashing him from side to side, / His bowels poured out upon the ground" (22.295–314). The remaining Spaniards, the canto tells us, are driven to the precipice, jumping to their doom: "all from the insecure summit / Did leap down and did hurl themselves / Blaming in vain and beyond any help / Their sad fortune and evil fate, / Sad, since before they struck the ground / They were dead from a hundred thousand blows / Upon the harsh and lofty rocks" (22.374–80).

Of course, this is a fiction of factual representation. The *Historia*'s ostensible chronicle function is a literary re-creation: Villagrá was nowhere near Acoma in early December. Rather he was riding back to la nueva México after having, at Oñate's orders, chased and executed two of the four September mutineers. We can assume that he must have been back in San Juan in late December when the survivors gave their accounts, since he was with the troop that attacked Acoma in January and was present at the trial in February when the surviving native people were tried and sentenced for their defiance. Indeed, he signed his name as witness to the February proceedings. Oñate had assigned Alonso Gómez Montesinos as defense attorney for the Acoma prisoners and then charged Villagrá to act as "guarantor" to ensure that Montesinos "would fulfill his oath and defend the Indians to the best of his ability." Should Montesinos "fail to do so, Villagrá, as his guarantor, accepted it as his own obligation and pledged to satisfy it with his own person and property."[22] Hence, Villagrá witnessed and must have noted all the testimonies describing what took place on December 4.

One of these testimonies provides us with a fascinating intertextual parallel to his poem. Bibero, who has his brains dashed by the old woman in the poem, is based on one of the soldiers, Martín de Biberos, who seems to have provoked the fatal incident at Acoma in December 1598. Alonso González, when asked "whether they caused any harm to the Indians of the pueblo," testified he "saw a soldier named Martín de Biberos holding a turkey in his hand and that an Indian woman was complaining about it [and] this took place at the time of the war cry."[23] That Villagrá seized upon this anecdote suggests that outside their lockstep testimonies, the Spanish must have talked about the incident, perhaps laying the tragedy to one man's stupidity. Of course, the soldier's casual theft functions as synecdoche for Spanish presumption throughout the New World. The poem also recalls the incident in the *Aeneid* in which the Trojan Ascanius kills Silvia's pet stag: "this the first cause of turmoil, kindling hearts / Of country folk to war" (7.663–64). In the *Historia*, just as in the *Aeneid*, one man's arrogant blunder unleashes the collective, pent-up rage of all the region's inhabitants. By imitating Virgil, Villagrá stages a single event to suggest how empire's ideological structures are alive and deadly dangerous in the individual subjects of the imperial state. The moment of crisis Villagrá narrates must be seen as either a disingenuous elision or a retrospective meditation on how, at Acoma, a single action led to vast destruction. The blundering, or malicious, action of a single individual is offered as the reason two nations went to war, if only because such facile reasoning gives a human face to those large social regimes that, however uneven militarily, are set on collision course. The Acoma attack the Spaniards because Biberos steals a turkey but also in retaliation against them for having wantonly taken corn, beans, blankets, and animals from Indian groups across the map of the Americas for a century.

Villagra's poetic sensibility, I suggest, was informed by his role as guarantor of the 1599 trial. This is not to argue that he sympathized with the Acoma. His own testimony possesses the rehearsed quality we see in other Spanish accounts and closes on a similarly punitive note: "he considers these Indians evil because they lived on such a stronghold." Villagrá, like the other witnesses, weirdly blamed Acoma's suicidal defiance on the invulnerability of their mesa stronghold. The pueblo, Villagrá explained, was "undermined with tunnels passing from house to house," and this is why "they were emboldened."[24] The other soldiers reiterate this account. Juan Medel, for example, testified that "Acoma is very strong . . . it was this fortress that induced them to kill the Spaniards, because if it had not been so strong they would now be at peace like the other pueblos."[25]

Years later, having seen Acoma's destruction up close, the poet's thinking shifted about how to represent the encounter. As guarantor, Villagrá was responsible for listening to the pueblo people's versions of what took place. None of the Acoma identify their fortress home as a catalyst for their risky defiance. Caucachi, one of the Acoma elders, not a fictional character, testified that the Spaniards had "wounded [a man] and for this reason his people became very angry and killed them," while another Acoma charged that the Spaniards "first killed an Indian" and were killed in return.[26] Perhaps these accounts haunted Villagrá years later, so that when he came to write the poem, he could not help but see the parallels among Troy, Numantia, and Acoma. It was not some perverse fortress mentality that caused their tragic destruction but foreign arrogance and brutality that unleashed a war of self-defense. As at Troy and Numantia, Acoma's mesa came to symbolize liberty. In the *Historia*, Villagrá figures native defiance, unyielding and sustained over centuries, in ways that give voice to his retrospective recognition that the Acoma had just cause for their resistance.

However divided by ideological ambivalence, the poet figures the final movement of the *Historia* with a dramatic force that surpasses his earlier announced focus upon the founding of la nueva México. Let me return to the poem's account of the first battle. Note a line I cited earlier, in which one of the Spanish soldiers has his brains bashed in by a "weak old woman" who is throwing stones from a housetop. If an old woman was participating in the battle, everyone in Acoma must have taken up arms against the Spanish. Villagrá figures her as a tribal elder who harbors deep historical knowledge of Spanish depredation. Her bold action is argument against the conciliatory gestures of Zutacapán's twenty-year-old son, Zutancalpo, who understood that armed uprising was futile but naively imagined that the Acoma and the Spanish could be friends. The elders knew the Spanish were not to be trusted. Stories about Coronado's violence half a century earlier had remained in circulation throughout the Pueblo world, and people knew that whatever friendship the Spaniards offered was predicated on their own submission.

Villagrá's turn to classical debate registers this understanding, yet the dilemma indigenous people faced when pressed by Spanish violence also marks the *Historia*'s otherwise predictable oratorical structure in the final cantos. Villagrá models Acoma debate on traditional European models, as Smith suggests, but he remained interested in the trial accounts for a content that bespeaks actual indigenous resolve beneath the stylized language. As one Acoma man, Xunista, testified: "Some wanted to make peace but others did not, and because they could not agree, they would not submit."[27] This testimony of tribal debate would have prompted Villagra's imaginative recuperation of council argument that without the trial record would be entirely contrived—a Spaniard's literary strategy to establish factitious dramatic tension for his readers. That there was probably tense discussion among the tribal elders about how to handle the crisis into which they were thrown allowed Villagrá to use earlier speech models to simultaneously vilify the pro-war faction, which Zutacapán represented, while offering praise to the accommodationists Chumpo and Zutalcapán. As the actual man Xunista reminded the author, though, "because they could agree, they would not submit," and so the tribal decision in 1598, born out of debate, not barbarous depravity, was to confront the Spaniards together, all. One of the Spaniards indeed testified that Acoma "men and women fought side by side from the terraces ... hurling stones and other missiles." When interrogated about why the women "threw rocks and helped in the fight," another Acoma man, Taxio, clarified the matter, saying "it was because they were together with the men."[28] For Zutacapán, a character in a fiction but one who articulates what we hear in the Acomans' testimonies, the issue is simple and stark: the Spaniards are thieves, and if they are allowed to summarily raid the storehouse, the Acoma will surely face a future of hunger, slavery, and subordination. Villagrá vilifies Zutacapán, but the words he puts into this character's mouth speak truth to empire.

~6~

In the poem, Villagrá structures the first show of resistance to Spanish arrogance as a battle between great warriors, but the actual event that took place on December 4, 1598, was no grand battle; rather the Spanish thieves were quickly dispatched. In the *Historia*, Villagrá transforms the skirmish into a monumental event. After single-handedly "spilling forth a whole sea of fresh blood" for three hours, Juan de Zaldívar, his thigh pierced by an arrow, becomes a "ravening lion" (rabioso león) who with "harsh howling and roars, mighty claws, and ravening teeth" battles all comers. Finally, however, Zutacapán wields his "furious mace" and strikes Zaldívar's "lofty temples," sending his enemy "to mortal rest and that long sleep / That need be all of us must sleep" (23.87–93). Zaldívar's corpse is set upon by the Acoma and, in a passage that recalls the desecration of Anaxarces in Laertius's *Lives* (IX), is ritually "ground up / In a great mortar, huge and stout, / Where in a sad and bloody paste / They left his body and his bones" (Adonde en lastimosa y tierna pasta / La carne y los güessos le dexaron) (23.119–22).[29]

This mimicry of classical descriptions of the fall of the great soldier is *puro cuento*, pure story, since the trial testimony of at least one of the Spanish survivors offers little more description of the contest than that they unceremoniously "struck the maese de campo with a stone and caused him to fall among some rocks."³⁰ What blurs history and epic topos emerges fully when another survivor recalls that after the battle the people "in the pueblo mockingly wore the hats and brandished the swords of the dead."³¹ In Villagrá this gives occasion to a scene in which Juan de Zaldívar's brother Vicente avenges his sibling's death by killing an Acoma warrior who is wearing Juan's clothing, a scene that in turn evokes Aeneas's rage at the sight of Turnus with Pallas's sword belt draped as an enemy token on his shoulder. For Villagrá, historical incident and epic strangely converged. Memory and mythos were brought near by the ancient poems he had read as a student in the University at Salamanca. Virgil's model enables Villagrá to make sense of what happened at Acoma, providing the Spanish writer with a stylized language that, as José Rabasa argues, aestheticizes violence.³²

Ten years after Oñate convened a "Trial of the Indians of the Pueblo of Acoma for having wantonly killed the Maese de Campo" (late December 1598) and then declared war on the pueblo, Villagrá chose to import into his own epic a legal document composed the week of the trial in which Oñate elicited from the *padres religiosos* a justification of war ("¿qué se require para la justificación de la guerra?").³³ The father commissary's response, a template document, seems out of place in the *Historia*. Why would Villagrá cut into the action of his poem by incorporating another long prose document? Inserting the clerical reply appears at first glance to distance him from culpability for the assault and massacre of the Acoma, a rhetorical decision that would bear out Rabasa's contention that Villagrá wrote the poem primarily to preclude charges against Oñate.³⁴ In fact, however, the clerical text exposes the priesthood's complicity in the massacre, perhaps even shifting responsibility for the war against the Acoma to the Church. The letter offers a point-by-point delineation of the justifications for war: to defend the innocent, recover property, punish delinquents, and, in the conventional linguistic contortion heard across the ages, "secure and preserve peace, for that is the principal end for which war is ordained."³⁵

Oñate declared a war of *sangre y fuego* on January 11, a week after receipt of fray Alonso Martínez's correspondence, "mandando pregonar, a sangre y fuego / Contra la fuerza de Acoma, la guerra." The text of Oñate's order requires the "people of Acoma to surrender the leaders of the uprising" and "abandon at once the fortified place in which they live and move down into the valley." Once they are removed, the soldiers are ordered to "burn it to the ground, and leave no stone on stone."³⁶ Villagrá essentially mimics the text of this declaration when he writes:

"Que, quemada la fuerza y abrasada, / A los culpados presos los truxesse" (And, razing and burning the fortress / He should bring back the guilty as prisoners) (25.93–94). The accompanying fathers sanction all these hard-willed actions. So much for stories about the padres' Christian sweetness and light. While he does not include the text of Oñate's punitive directive, the poet nevertheless makes explicit the general's harsh order in the closing lines of the twenty-fifth canto.

Villagrá must have known that to import too much prose (especially legalese) would ruin the poem, but the interpolation yokes his verse account of the impending massacre to official documents that make clear the priests' and Oñate's joint culpability. The poet's earlier incorporation of the long act of possession in canto fourteen, as I have suggested, exposes Oñate and the entire chain of authority, including the King, for their power-grabbing manipulation of the colonists. Likewise here, for when we read lines that clarify Oñate's order to burn the pueblo, take all the Acoma prisoner, "Sin que chico ni grande se escapase" (Without one, great or small, escaping), and then, take some of those of "edad entera" (fully mature adults) to make "un exemplar castigo de manera / Que todos los demás con tal enmienda / Quedasen para siempre escarmentados" (an exemplary punishment, so that all the rest, at such indemnity, might take a warning for all time) (25.105–10), we are squarely confronted with the precise measure of Spanish cruelty the Acoma remember today. The poem, closing with battle in the traditional style, does not end with or even mention the trial at which the beleaguered Acoma people, upon Oñate's sentence, are put into servitude, torn asunder, their children sent off to Mexico, their surviving warriors forced to suffer amputation. This *castigo* set a bitter foundation for the Pueblo Revolt of 1680, and it is one the Acoma people recall today when, for example, the guide points out the small openings in the adobe wall surrounding their cemetery through which the spirits of their abducted children, still mourned by the pueblo, will return.

Because the author-character summarily falls back on earlier literary models to abstract historical events in which he participated, he blurs history and fiction, offering classical topos as a frame for those events. For Villagrá as for writers of New World epic generally, the script of history simultaneously provides a space for celebrating empire and for sorting through the wreckage left in its wake. Oñate had already decided he would destroy Acoma, but, Villagrá writes, the detailed "escritos graves" (clerical documents) the priests delivered sealed his right and responsibility on the violent retribution he intended. Villagrá here invokes Aeneas's journey to consult the Sibyl to affirm his decision to conquer the Latin people. Just as Virgil's contemporary readers would have recalled the emperor's manipulation of the priesthood (especially those guardians of the Sibylline books, the priesthood of fifteen, or *quindecimviri sacris faciundis*) to justify another war, so too Villagrá's classically trained readers would have regarded his move with a certain irony. Rather than providing aesthetic distance, this strategy invited them to look more closely at the historical record and sort through its obfuscations.

Canto twenty-six offers a companion piece to the Spanish war council, picking up in Acoma after the Spanish have been thrown over the cliff. The canto mirrors the preceding narrative in which Oñate measures the colonists' support of his grave intention and then, to seal his intent, consults the apostolic commissary and the friars. We see two factions: "valiant," clear-minded Indians (26.12) and raging, unreasoning "barbarians" (26.50). Giocombo, figured as "un bárbaro valiente" (26.12) with his great friend, the Apache Bempol, "Valiente por extremo y gran soldado" (26.33), is leading discussion with other "bárbaros valientes" (26.50) on the merits of going to war against the Spanish. These tribal leaders are figured as the equivalent of Virgil's council of elders. After debate and flaring tempers, the council leaders are "three against three" (26.206) on how to proceed and turn to Amulco, the Acoma wizard ("un hechizero") (26.211), who, like the Sybil, speaks with the deities who intervene in the affairs of men.

In a trance, Amulco travels to the underworld, then tells the war council that their spy, Qualco, reported during the Spanish demonstration of military strength at Ohkay Owingeh how "estos mismos Castillas" (26.259) fired their guns at each other without felling a single man. "Their weapons," Qualco concludes, "were no more than fright alone / A clamorous noise, fearful horror, / And, finally, all sound, for their lightnings" (26.264–66). If only that had been true. The enactment he refers to is *Moros y Cristianos*, the drama that, as I have outlined in the previous chapter, was part of the repertoire of power the Spaniards staged to terrorize native people into quiescence. Amulco justifies warfare for the Acoma, assuring everyone that "The sun is not so sure to give us light / As it is sure we shall have victory" (26.304–5). Giocombo offers a different interpretation: the Spaniards did not die because "like gods / They fight and nothing injures them" (26.273–75). Both notions are the poet's contrivance, of course, but they allow Villagrá to represent native resistance in a classical parallel familiar to his readers.

When he invokes the characters and oratory of classical and New World epic, Villagrá pays intertextual tribute to earlier authors at the same time that he contrives indigenous world views in speeches that sound conspicuously European. Bruce Smith dismisses this oratory with rhetorical questions: "Why take the trouble of granting the Indians voices? Why invent speeches for them?"[37] The answer, of course, is that epic requires a dialogic structure to bring cultural difference and antagonism to immediacy through speech. Smith answers his own queries when he refers to this epic topos in the writings of Herodotus and Thucydides, who also fashioned oratory for the principal characters in their histories. History, after all, is simply another genre of storytelling through which we come to understand the past. Given its European discursive antecedents, Villagrá's refashioning of native speech, needless to say, reads as artificial and racist. Having owned as much, though, it still seems important to insist that he and other New World writers of the sixteenth and seventeenth centuries exploit the only discourses they have available to them to confront their ambivalence about native people.

In the *Historia*, Villagrá layers these uncertainties, questions, and anxieties about an indigenous world whose coherent social structures, hunting culture, and kindness he has been at pains to honor in the early cantos. His voicing of indigenous speech is a distortion, yes, but what else can we expect? The question I prefer to ask is this: what can we learn about this Spaniard's negotiation of imperial relations through his speech contrivances? While Villagrá is clearly performing empire's puppet show, he permits his marionettes to say things that make me wonder what the Acoma must have thought when they saw, from their blessed home, a troop of Spanish soldiers riding across the spacious valley toward them. I wonder, too, what coursed through the soldiers' minds as they who rode toward the fortress in the sky they had been ordered to destroy.

Villagrá provokes disquiet as he describes the encounter. When Oñate's troops finally arrive at Acoma, Villagrá describes the angry, defiant people who shout and flaunt themselves from the high cliffs. The Spanish author notes the women and children who join in defying the invaders, once again representing resistance as widespread:

> Una grandiosa suma nunca vista
> De bárbaras bizarras, muy hermosas,
> Las partes bergonzosas enseñando
> A vuestros Castellanos, confiadas
> De la victoria cierta que esperaban.
> También, entre varones y mugeres,
> Andaban muchos bárbaros desnudos,
> Los torpes miembros todos descubiertos,
> Tiznados y embijados de unas rayas
> Tan espantables, negras y grimosas
> Qual si demonios bravos del infierno
> Fueran, con sus melenas, desgreñados,
> Y colas arrastrando y unos cuernos
> Desmesurados, gruessos y crecidos. (27.166–79)

(A large group as was never before seen of / Spirited barbarian women, very beautiful, / Displaying their shameful parts / To the Castilians, confident / Of the certain victory they awaited. / Also, among men and women, / There were many naked barbarians / Their unchaste members fully displayed / Sooty and painted with broad streaks, / As fearful, black, and horrible, / As if they were brave demons out of hell / With long, loose hair all disheveled / And wearing tails and also horns / Immeasurable, long and huge; / And in this dress, all without shame, / They leaped like deer among the rocks, / Shouting to us in words very defiant.)

This stanza, which demonizes the Acoma and undoubtedly was intended to evoke astonished reaction from his contemporary readers, is mostly a fiction. Some of the Spanish testimonies, including Villagrá's, note that when they arrived at the mesa, the Acoma were waiting at the precipice to taunt them, but there is no mention of the costuming or nakedness about which we read in the poem. Villagrá testified that the Indians "uttered loud shouts and outcries, showed great joy at the sight of the Spaniards, and pelted them with arrows, wooden javelins, and chunks of ice."[38] In both accounts, the Acoma seem prepared for battle, but their theatrics suggest they hoped to avoid war by scaring the Spanish away using their own arsenal of fearful images, images not unlike those of the theater of terror the Spanish had used since 1519.

Nearly a century later, Villagrá has the Acoma defy the soldiers using the very fetishes of fear that Christian theology imposed upon Europe over the centuries—nakedness, shameful after the fall of Adam and Eve—demonic figures wearing tails and horns, hovering in every corner of the Christian imagination, which the Church repeatedly invoked to keep its subjects in submission through fear-inducing medieval morality plays, the torturous images of Inquisition sermons, and the interrogations and torture to exorcise demons of doubt. As a character in his own poem, Villagrá, a loyal subject and good Roman Catholic, would frame the scene accordingly. Whether fully intended or not, his chaos of barbarism and frightening figures holds in tension the competing cultural and ideological figurations that had long disturbed the Spanish imagination.

Villagrá parrots the party line: seventy gallant soldiers look up to the cliff fortress high above where the "demonios bravos del infierno," displaying their shameful parts, produce both fear and resolve. Yet, years after this battle, while he sat at his writing table in Madrid, or perhaps earlier, when he rode away from la nueva México never to return, the weight of his arrogance and regret perhaps settled on him—else why recall the native display of anger, pride, and war readiness with such attention to their knowing theatrics? From this scene to the poem's close, the immense sin of massacre pulls against the poem's official story like an undertow. Figuring the Acoma as demonic in this scene simply cannot undo the later horror of their bodies piled high, their blood bathing the walls of the mesa. Villagrá retrospectively structures the Acoma ritual defiance as a theater of burlesque that must be read against the *Moros y Cristianos* performance the Acoma spies had witnessed in early September. What the soldiers watch on the cliff could have been no less strange than when the Acoma spies beheld the odd jousting matches, the roaring of blank shots fired from harquebus and cannon, and the weird fighting among men dressed in flowing gowns with Moorish turbans. These Spaniards, performing themselves in steel-sharp helmets and full body armor of hammered metal, mounted on horses breast-plated and masked, played their own strange role in the whirling charge of noise. Cheering them on were the women and children, not women nearly naked but worse, gaudily covered from neck to toe with heavy material, their own armor against the devil's whispers. Native people must have found this display appalling and ridiculous.

In the poem, Acoma's theatrical defiance works: Oñate's settler soldiers are terrified. In one of his occasional appearances in the narrative, Villagrá is called upon to prevent Zaldívar's vengeance-driven assault on the mesa:

> Temiendo se perdiesse todo el resto,
> Algunos me pidieron que tratase
> Con el dicho Sargento que advirtiesse
> Aquello que intentaba y no arresgase
> Cosa tan importante y que pedía
> Acuerdo muy maduro y muy pesado,
> Porque en saliendo mal de aquel intento
> Era fuerza perderse y assolarse.
> Y dándole razón de todo aquesto
> Y de otras muchas cosas que passamos,
> Tomando mal aquello que propuse,
> Sin más considerar, me dixo ayrado:
> "Yo trazaré esta causa de manera
> Que más no me repliquen estas dueñas (28.45–58)

(Some asked me that I should try / To warn the sergeant against / That which he intended and not risk / So important a thing without seeking / Agreement more mature and weighty, / For if things were to turn out badly / All would certainly be lost and destroyed / And, offering rationale for this / And for many other things we discussed / But taking badly what I proposed / Without any consideration, he told me angrily: / "I will carry out this cause in such manner / That these housewives cannot refute" [translation mine].)

The soldiers are afraid. To keep them in line, Zaldívar insults their manhood. Villagrá makes himself a spokesman for men justifiably suspicious of Zaldívar's motives; men who had hoped for more deliberation and wondered at Oñate's own absence from the assault. There is much disquiet about Oñate ("otras muchas cosas que passamos") (28.54) tightly concealed within a single line that discloses the deep faction that exists within the colony. Oñate, governor and general, should, like Aeneas, have led his men into battle, but counseled by the priests and "todo el Real" (25.32) (the colonists) he stayed behind. Apologetically prolix elsewhere, Villagrá chooses to suppress the debate that must have ensued, writing only, "Ubo sobre este acuerdo grandes cosas / Muy largas de contar" (About this matter there was debate too complicated / And too long to tell) (25.29–30). We already know that disenchantment with Oñate's leadership had been brewing before the group's arrival in la nueva México. Like readers in 1610, I cannot help but assume that Villagrá gestures here toward the colony's apprehension that Oñate would botch the military campaign. Zaldívar preempts debate, however, silencing the men—"'Aquí no ay qué tratar'" (There is nothing to discuss)—and calling them "dueñas," or housewives. Yet at the canto's close it is a dueña ("doña Eufemia, valerosa") (27.275) who, back in San Juan, rallies the women to mount the rooftops and as much as orders Oñate "que solas las dexasen" (27.280) (to "leave them alone") to defend the colony. Just as Villagrá time and again represents the soldiers suffering deprivation at every turn for King and country, he honors Acoma's women and implicitly derogates Oñate's failure to lead either the battle of Acoma or the defense of the colonial settlement. In scripting the heroics of these women, Villagrá obliquely refutes Oñate's authority. Like the historical Oñate, who was indeed losing his grip on the colony, Villagrá's governor cedes heroic status to the "fuerte hombros del Sargento" (the mighty shoulders of Sergeant Zaldívar) and as much as disappears from the poem.

Today, looking up at Acoma, my head tilts at an uncomfortable angle. I face a stark, sheer wall of desert stone and wonder how the Spaniards ever scaled this cliff. In 1598 it could be climbed only through one narrow passageway, which, guarded, blocked all ascent. While the main troop mounted a diversion at the northwest point of access, though, Zaldívar sent twelve soldiers—Villagrá among them—to the southern cliff, where under cover of darkness they wedged themselves under a ledge. When the Acoma rallied to defend the fortress from the army below, these twelve men climbed unnoticed to its top and opened fire from the rear. If Villagrá likens Acoma elsewhere to Masada or Numantia, here he makes only tacit allusion to Spanish military strategy learned from the Romans who had scaled fortresses in Gaul, Britain, the Middle East, and ancient Iberia. Homer celebrates the cunning strategies of Ulysses, who thinks up the masterful deceit of the gift horse that ruins Troy. Villagrá, by comparison, makes only glancing reference to his own role in the battle. Here Villagrá figures himself as one of the least able of the twelve soldiers. As with the vulnerability and fear he projects in the episode where he loses his horse and kills his dog in an act of desperation, he diminishes his role in the military exploits he celebrates as he names each of his fellow soldiers: "aquellos bravos . . . / y yo con ellos / Que assí fue necessario porque el colmo / No fuesse tan cumplido y que mermase" (those brave men . . . and I with them / So that their greatness would be diminished and lessened) (29.20–34).

The *Historia*'s editors note that "Villagrá again, in narrating his own presence, strikes the exaggeratedly humble pose expected."[39] While I do not disagree, there is nonetheless something heroic about his refusal to boast of his exploits here and elsewhere, as, for example, when later in the battle, he leaps across a deep chasm without waiting for orders to reset a log that allows a gush of soldiers into the pueblo. What Villagrá does not indicate in the poem is that this very action proved the turning point against any possibility of victory for the Acoma. From this moment it was only a matter of hours before the pueblo was destroyed. False humility perhaps, but as poet-scribe, his description of the slaughter that ensued at Acoma calls into question David J. Weber's note that "the small Spanish army of seventy-two men achieved a brilliant victory."[40] In singing of arms and the man, he merely recalls himself slashing, shooting, and eviscerating people. Poetry aestheticizes massacre, yes, but Villagrá's poetics of violence does not allow readers to forget massacre. Four hundred years later, the *Historia* continues to remind us what the cultural preservationists would like to forget.

Villagrá describes a killing field no less gruesome than those in Homer and Virgil. Earlier in the canto, Villagrá speaks out of the other side of his mouth when he renders Zaldívar as a classical hero urging his men on by reminding them that as newly entitled hidalgos they must fight valiantly for Spain. These grand words ring empty a few lines later, though, when we read of the slaughter these gentleman soldiers leave behind. The Acoma are fierce in battle, but predictably doomed in a war of wooden maces against steel, arrows against guns:

> Y viendo al enemigo tan a pique,
> Los nuestros todos juntos dispararon
> Los prestos arcabuzes, y aunque a muchos
> Por tierra derribaron, fueles fuerza,
> Por no poderles dar segunda carga,
> Venir a las espadas y, rebueltos
> Los unos con los otros. . . .
> Soterrando las dagas y los filos
> De las vivas espadas, grande gifa
> De miserables cuerpos destrozados
> Y un matadero horrendo ya tenían. . . .

CHAPTER 3

> Y abriendo grandes fuentes, derramaron
> Por los bárbaros pechos y costados
> Ojos, cabezas, piernas y gargantas
> De fresca sangre arroyos caudalosos
> Por cuis bravas bocas espantosas
> Las almas temerosas presta fuga. (30.141–75)

(Seeing the enemy so near / Our men, in a volley, fired / Their ready harquebuses, and though many / Fell dead to the earth, they were forced / Unable to load a second time, / To come to swords, and in the heat of battle / They mixed in armed combat.... / Plunging their daggers and the sharp edges / Of their swift swords in a great slaughter / Of miserable, shattered bodies / They made a horrendous butchery.... / opening great wounds, they / Shed from the barbarian breasts and ribs / Eyes, heads, and legs, and throats, / Gushing streams of their fresh blood, / From their courageous and frightened mouths / Their fearful souls did take swift flight.)

Perhaps Villagrá tricked himself into telling the truth. "I'll write a learned soldier's epic harking to Virgil, to Homer, celebrating our adventure in that far off place and time," he might have thought, only to find that the more he wrote, the more he saw into the heart of what he had done as a soldier. Then perhaps he woke in the middle of the night, returned to the writing table, and in the scratch of quill saw and heard again up close the violence he and his fellows had committed ten years before. Though the lines recall the charged, traditional language of epic battle, they immediately make apparent, unlike those poems of ancient warfare, that this battle is a travesty. In classic stories, valor in battle was premised on equals fighting equals: sword against sword. The "matadero horrendo" (horrendous butchering) Villagrá depicts visualizes guns bringing down clusters of warriors and then represents hand-to-hand combat as a charade of wooden clubs against unyielding, lethal steel. So many Acoma are slaughtered that the walls of the mesa he recalls are "bañado y sangretado" (31.26)—bathed and soaked in blood. The nightmare of killing will not stop, though. The Acoma, courageous and enraged, charge squarely into the "boca de cañón" (31.35)—the very mouth of the muskets firing round upon round of death-scattering lead ("soberbias balas" 31.37). As though the reverie of death from sword and harquebus were not enough, the Spaniards lift two artillery pieces to the mesa battlefield and fire at another "three hundred brave, furious" (31.71) Acoma warriors, who, Villagrá writes, are killed like a flock of magpies hit with buckshot. I quote at length:

> De presto las dos piezas regoldaron,
> Cada, dozientos clavos y, con esto
> Qual suelen las hurracas que, espantadas,
> Suspenden los chirridos y grasnidos
> Con la fuerza de pólvora que arroja
> De munición gran copia, con que vemos
> Escaper a las unas y a las otras
> Quedar perniquebradas y otras muertras
> Y otras barriendo el suelo con las alas,
> El negro pico abierto y con las tripas
> Arrastrando, rasgadas las entrañas,
> No de otra suerte, juntos todos vimos
> De súbito, gran suma de difuntos
> Tullidos, mancos, cojos, destroncados.
> Abiertos por los pechos, mal heridos,
> Rasgadas las cabezas y los brazos,
> Abiertos por mil partes y las carnes
> Vertiendo viva sangre, agonizando,
> Las inmortales almas despedían
> Dexando allí los cuerpos palpitando. (31.74–93)

(Suddenly the two artillery pieces belched / Two hundred spikes from each, and / Just as we see the magpies, terrorized, / Suspend their chirping and their cackling / At the charge of powder which scatters / Great mass of small shot, and we see / A few escaping and the others / Left with shattered limbs, many others dead, / With others sweeping broken wings across the ground / Their black beaks agape and their bowels / Pouring forth from out their torn bellies / We then had no other choice, but to see, all of us / A great heap of the dead / Mangled, hands severed, legs gone, shattered / Deep gashes in their chests, deep wounds / Their heads torn open, their arms / Pierced a thousand times, their flesh / Pouring out living blood, in mortal agony / Their immortal souls taking leave / Leaving their bodies quivering there [translation mine].)

The lines render battle as butchery, this soldier recalling the excoriation of the Acoma warriors who, defending their homes, are brought down like mere birds by Spanish weaponry. Villagrá's images of men reduced to magpies with shattered wings and gaping beaks certainly dehumanizes the Acoma warriors, but his metaphor offers readers an unforgettable correlative of the savage inequality of the battle: what should be epic warfare is reduced to a bird shoot. A line later, the Acoma are restored to their essential humanity, broken wings and beaks agape turned back into shattered legs and heads torn open. The visual field of the poem gives the sense of a Hieronymus Bosch painting where men and animal images merge in nightmarish anguish or reminds us of Ovid's metamorphosed figures shimmering between human and animal form. The poem here offers a powerful representation of the surreal horror of warfare for those men who carry out empire's fatal mission. Villagrá the soldier recalls what Virgil can merely imagine: "No de otra suerte, juntos todos vimos" (31.85)—we had no other choice, all of us saw, we were doomed to see, it was our collective punishment to witness this "great heap of the dead" (31.86). The Spanish soldiers seem to stop in midsentence to behold the surreal deathscape they have made. His images of mangled and shattered bodies are shaped by a long epic tradition, yet here Villagrá uses classical literature precisely to make graphic the slaughter and "mortal agony" the Acoma people suffered in January 1599. There is no such explicit account in any of the reports from Oñate describing the massacre.

Did they—Villagrá and other besmirched Spaniards—see immortal souls rising from those palpitating bodies in their death shudders? Or is this simply a shopworn trope repeated for dramatic effect? Perhaps both: Roman Catholic habit, a way of apprehending the release of the soul from the dying body, and literary strategy, a means for representing war on a human scale, converging in the lines with the force of self-revelation the poet may not himself fully recognize. A few lines earlier the Acoma are presented as "perros bravos" (31.42), fierce dogs, but now they are fully human in their "mortal agony," possessed of the life spirit Villagrá here and elsewhere suggests indigenous people possess just as much as his Christian compatriots. The canto is replete with emotional and ideological oscillation in which the poet alternately celebrates Spanish bravery and Acoma courage, offering heroic speeches from Zaldívar and the valiant rhetoric of Giacombo, and then closing with an appalling scene of the pueblo's destruction to the letter of Oñate's order: "leave no stone on stone."[41]

I read troubled recollection here, contravened by the imperial bias that structures epic while memory torques heroic refrain. I also read adumbrative guilt within these ambivalent tropes in an act that may be interpreted either as foolhardy, given the legal case being built against Oñate and his lieutenants after 1605, or as courageous moral reckoning. Villagrá names the very men—Cortés, Francisco Sánchez, Pedraza, Ribera, Juan Medel, Alonzo Sánchez, and others—who went through the pueblo, torches in hand, setting "on fire some of the houses there / To frighten them" (31.156–57). The poem offers nothing valiant or heroic in the torching of a village already desecrated and piled with hundreds of dead men and women—and children. Indeed, the *Historia* exposes the reign of terror aimed against the soul of the pueblo itself, its dwellings burning, the habitations that had housed generations of Acoma people billowing into fire and smoke: "Todas las tristes casas calentando. . . . / Bolando hazia el Cielo despedían / Gran suma de centellas y de chispas" (All the sad houses, / Spewing up to Heaven / A great mass of embers and hot coals) (31.241–51).

Knowing the chronicle of the pueblo's destruction is crucial to reading the poem here. Villagrá imitates Virgil's description of the razing of Troy, but his mimicry does not exaggerate the destruction wrought here. When Homer wrote the *Iliad*, the Trojan War was already an ancient tale; Virgil's account, removed from this battle by another thousand years, is pure myth. In 1610, only ten years after being burned to the ground, Acoma was still smoldering, its surviving citizens dispersed. I cannot help but seize upon the anguish resident in a single phrase "tristes casas calentando"—having absorbed the life spirit of people and community over hundreds of years, the pueblo houses are figured as feeling entities brought to a sad end. Some eight hundred people—five hundred men and three hundred women and children—were killed over three days, their homes destroyed. In the short space of two or three days only a single Spaniard was killed—by friendly fire. So much for a heroic battle between equals and for what the historian David J. Weber recently referred to as a "brilliant victory."[42]

Those pueblo inhabitants who had not thrown themselves over the cliff or run back into the burning flames refusing to surrender were rounded up—some five hundred women and children and only eighty surviving men—marched down the mesa and across the desert to another pueblo sixty miles away where they were put on trial. The poem closes not by chronicling the humiliating kangaroo court and the demeaning sentence Oñate imposed upon them on February 12—the women and most of the young were dispersed among the colonists for twenty years of servitude, scores of children were sent off to convents in Mexico, and men older than twenty-five were forced to have one foot cut off so as to be hobbled during their own twenty-year enslavement. It instead dramatizes an act of defiance by two Acoma men.

One may argue that Villagrá exploits conventional epic closure to gloss over this degrading treatment of the surviving Acoma people. Had he chosen to detail the dispersal of the tribe and focus on the amputation of the men's feet, however, his account would hardly have raised a seventeenth-century eyebrow. As David J. Weber notes, severing limbs was "an acceptable punishment for miscreants in Renaissance Europe" and, as he continues, "not unique to Spaniards in America." Weber writes that at "the fledgling English colony of Jamestown, Thomas Gates had the hand of an Indian cut off as a warning against spies.... Nor did those early English settlers spare women and children from harsh reprisals. Jamestown colonists punished some Powhatan children, taken captive in 1610, by throwing them off a ship and 'shoteinge owtt their Braynes in the water.'"[43] My point is not to offer a rationalization for such European savagery, but to suggest that Villagrá chooses a traditional epic curse against the victors with which to close the poem—two Acoma men hang themselves rather than concede—to show that their defiance and will to freedom could not be broken, even after the pueblo and its people were devastated.

This staged suicide is intended to draw a recognizable parallel between his poem and those classics upon which he modeled the *Historia* that cannot but evoke lingering discomfort. David Quint argues that for Villagrá and his seventeenth-century readers, the defiant suicide "is a projection of their dread of future Indian revolts and retribution—and, hence, in some sense a veiled expression of their feelings of guilt—[yet] it also justifies, with the logic of the vicious circle, the severity of their present policy."[44] As for the first part of Quint's equation: what was there to dread? Almost a thousand Acoma people had been slaughtered and only one Spaniard had died—and none of the other pueblos joined the Acoma resistance. Dread resided in Indian country. Other pueblos had abandoned their homes as soon as they saw the Spaniards approaching, or they humbled themselves, watching as their supplies were stolen, averted eyes focusing only on the future, on survival. When the poem was published, I would argue, there could have been little concern about native uprising. Open defiance would have to brew for nearly another century. As for offering justification for Spanish mendacity, I would be tempted to assert that the

Spaniards seldom worried greatly about justifying their violence against native people. Although the *leyes de las Indias* warned against harming native people with threats of severe punishment and even execution, Spanish murderers were rarely brought to trial. If they were, punishment was seldom severe. Remember that Oñate, Zaldívar, and Villagrá himself were convicted of brutality against Acoma, but not one of these men served a day in prison. On the contrary, they were exiled from a world to which they never intended to return for its utter failure to produce the gilded vision they originally imagined.

Their guilt is another matter. In the *Historia*, justification and culpability are set forever at odds in an epic that exposes the mechanics of empire even as it reveals to the careful reader the effects of Spanish cruelty on Villagrá himself. The poet's searing images of slaughter, his startling picture of magpies scattered by the deadly recoil of cannon shot, his recollection of the pueblo burning, his description of the Acomans' "sad homes ablaze, smoke rising into the sky" all suggest a complex set of emotions: melancholy, empathy, regret, and self-censure. Yet readers like Quint, for whom Villagrá's *Historia* remains a "poem of small literary merit," merely "doggerel verse," dismiss and foreclose upon Villagrá's ability to write a poem of intellectual and moral complexity sufficient to recognize and symbolically weigh the mendacities perpetrated by the empire in which he soldiered. Presumably this soldier, a hack without poetic skill or imagination, such readers presume, was capable only of writing an uncritical celebration of the expedition to la nueva México. Such interpretations ignore the fact that, well before he wrote the closing curse, Villagrá had declared his impatience with, or abhorrence of, Oñate (and in a very real, if veiled, sense with the King) by refusing to return to la nueva México only months after the massacre. Yes, of course, years later he would lap up to the court yet again to win a post in the Americas, but it remains incontrovertible that in 1599 he abandoned Oñate's fairy-tale expedition, sullied, as the poem shows, by the murder of fellow soldiers and his part in a massacre. Villagrá's disloyalty, it seems to me, produces a visceral closure that reveals his own unresolved sentiments about the expedition and the battle at Acoma, just as it aligned with charges of cruelty the colonists themselves made against Oñate.

The curse provided a well-known epic trope that on its surface would not trouble court censors. It brought an already very long poem to a close without chronicling the trial, but not without gesturing figuratively at the faction it caused within the Spanish colony, and curtly ended with another nightmarish scene of two Acoma men hanging themselves from a cottonwood tree, their bodies a haunting reminder of those mangled heaps of dead villagers who had dared defy Spain. Yes, the two men were actually hanged at Oñate's orders, but in the poem Villagrá proffers symbolic agency and in so doing a Spaniard concedes the spiritual sovereignty of this mesa people. When one visits Acoma today it is clear that the people have gathered their lives around their own understanding of Haakú, a place prepared for them long in advance of the Spanish invasion and promised to them for a long future. Something in Villagrá's representation of Acoma's defiance envisions not Quint's "future of scattered suicidal gestures, ultimately without aim or direction," but the futility of empire's attempt to reduce indigenous people to dispirited subjects.[45] Even after Padre Ramírez coaxed them into building a huge church atop their mesa in the 1630s, they retained their religious and cultural sovereignty, first by maintaining ritual in secret from the prying Spaniards and then by honoring their faith openly as the centuries ensued, when another empire washed over the land that would become the American Southwest. This resolve remains apparent when one visits San Esteban del Rey Mission and notes the mural figures of native cornstalks, clouds, and rainbows adorning the interior mission walls. The most arresting figures are the parrot designs, one on each side of the altar, alert and watchful.

By 1610 Villagrá might well have heard that the people he had helped butcher had started to return. What he could not have known, however, was that the Acoma people would gather with Po'pay, the Ohkay Owingeh leader, to resist the Spanish yet again in 1680. Quint presumably would label this later rebellion another "suicidal gesture," since the Spanish returned twelve years later to reconquer the territory. But I have yet to read or hear an Indian concede that 1680 was an action "without aim or direction." In the centuries since Po'pay led his audacious uprising, the Acoma and other indigenous groups have suffered repeated violence and humiliation, but they have remained steadfast in their refusal to surrender their place in the world. Even today, native people have neither forgotten nor forgiven Oñate's order. When the Spanish preservationists erected heroic statues to their "conquistador," in January 1998 someone symbolically avenged the ancient cruelty visited upon Acoma by amputating Oñate's bronze foot outside of Ohkay Owingeh.[46] The Acoma people today number more than twenty-eight hundred, and they remain stewards of their magnificent "white rock" and the surrounding country of some 380,000 acres. They remain steadfast in their traditions and lifeways, while also negotiating the realities of life in the twenty-first century. Villagrá's *Historia de la Nueva Mexico*, an epic of empire, closes in a scene of native defiance, which over time, as the Acoma tour guide reminds us, has deepened their resolve to remain atop Haakú for another thousand years.

Epilogue

~ 1 ~

Let me close with an imagined narrative exchange between Esperanza López, or Hope, as my mother was renamed in grade school by los americanos, and Simon J. Ortiz, or Hihdruutsi, which is how the famous poet is known in Acoma.

My mother has been sitting at the kitchen table—almost literally—for the few years I have been writing this book. She has read the *Historia* along with essays here and chapters there of nearly all I myself have read about this long poem. She will not read anything if I ask her to, but if I strategically leave books and papers lying about she will read until well past midnight. I know she will have an opinion on whatever she picks up. We have talked and talked about what took place in 1598 and in the years that followed Spain's settlement in la nueva México. While she is proud of her Nuevomexicano heritage, my mother is angry at los españoles. Across the house from where I write about Villagrá's poem in another room, I hear her say to herself, to the walls, to the past, and to me, "Pobre gente, ¿por qué les hiciéron así? I am so ashamed of what happened there." She tells me of her pride in New Mexico—"mi país"—but at the same time of her anger and chagrin at reading this epic story of a massacre "there." She has visited Acoma during Christmas, when the pueblo is open to everyone and people are invited into individual homes to eat. She remembers the people she met as effusive in their welcome. I fill in the story. The Acoma people—those five hundred who survived—were forced down from the mesa and marched to what came to be called Santo Domingo Pueblo, where they were subjected to trial for treason and murder. "Treason?" she asks. "What did they do but defend themselves?" I tell her about the men who had their feet severed and the children who were sent to Mexico. I read Oñate's sentence to her. The look she gives when I finish is haunted, and haunting. She as much as orders me, "Print his order for everyone to know what he did. All these years I thought he was a good man, pero era muy estúpido y muy cruel." Here, then, is the order Oñate delivered in February 1599. It stands in my book as another kind of commemorative against the regal bronzes.

In the criminal case between the royal court and the Indians of the pueblo and fortress of Acoma ... accused of having wantonly killed don Juan de Zaldívar Oñate, maese de campo general of this expedition, and Captains Felipe de Escalante and Diego Núñez, eight soldiers, and two servants, and of other crimes; and in addition to this, after Vicente de Zaldívar Mendoza, my sargento mayor, whom I sent for this purpose in my place, had repeatedly called upon them to accept peace, not only did they refuse to do so, but actually received him with hostility, wherefore, taking into account the merits of the case and the guilt resulting therefrom, I must and do sentence all of the Indian men and women from the said pueblo under arrest, as follows:

The males who are over twenty-five years of age I sentence to have one foot cut off and to twenty years of personal servitude.

The males between the ages of twelve and twenty-five I sentence likewise to twenty years of personal servitude.

The women over twelve years of age I sentence likewise to twenty years of personal servitude.

Two Indians from the province of Moqui who were present at the pueblo of Acoma and who fought and were apprehended, I sentence to have the right hand cut off and to be set free in order that they may convey to their land the news of this punishment.

All the children under twelve years of age I declare free and innocent of the grave offense for which I punish their parents. And because of my duty to aid, support, and protect both the boys and girls under twelve years of age, I place the girls under the care of our father commissary, Fray Alonso Martínez, in order that he, as a Christian and qualified person, may distribute them in this kingdom or elsewhere in monasteries or other places where he thinks that they may attain the knowledge of God and the salvation of their souls.

The boys under twelve years of age I entrust to Vicente de Zaldívar Mendoza, my sargento mayor, in order that they may attain the same goal.

The old men and women, disabled in the war, I order freed and entrusted to the Indians of the province of the Querechos that they may support them and may not allow them to leave their pueblos.

I order that all of the Indian men and women who have been sentenced to personal servitude shall be distributed among my captains and soldiers in the manner which I will prescribe and who may hold and keep them as their slaves for the said term of twenty years and no more.

This being a definite and final sentence, I so decree and order,

Don Juan de Oñate (February 12, 1599)[1]

~ 2 ~

She who nears the end of her own history, Esperanza, then listens as I read a contemporary Acoma poet. Simon J. Ortiz is a Native American poet who measures the devastation of this first encounter and in language unfaltering and bold projects a future continuous with, not defeated by, its past. In the clutch of "Acoma Poems" in *Out There Somewhere* (2002), Ortiz writes that his people shall keep moving into the future by "looking back to the past" to "see how our peoples in the past lived / how they were guided, how they lived well."[2] His poem, "This is the Way Still We Shall Go On" acknowledges that "It is necessary to look back to the past," not through a shrinking reflection that loses itself to the nightmare Villagrá scribed four hundred years ago, but to a future "guided by . . . the way of living that will be correct and good for us" (92). The poem bespeaks a long and poised tribal knowledge, unbroken by devastation, in which an idea of "correct" living must not be abandoned to dread, fear, or anger.

The Spanish left not a stone on stone in 1599. They—we—killed hundreds of men, women, and children and dispersed hundreds more. Yet, the core life of Haakú remained vital: "Even when it's chopped down its center core stays green and alive. / It will grow again many years later. It never dies. It keeps living." ("Histories, Places, Indians, Just Like Always," 40).[3] After twenty years of removal, Haakú, that place prepared for Ortiz and his people, as much as breathed, "green and alive." Stone was placed back upon stone in the years after 1620 so that "many years later" the pueblo would "grow again" into the soaring sky city it is today.

In "For the Children," Ortiz invokes the dread memory of those innocents who, after the destruction of their pueblo, were taken away to convents and missions in Mexico to, as Oñate ordered, "attain the knowledge of God and the salvation of their souls." Villagrá himself conveyed many of these girl children when he was ordered to return to Mexico for more recruits. Carried south, they "never returned"; grew, and withered, within a confinement of Church and empire. Apparitions now, yet never forgotten. Villagrá's closing curse is both a trope of empire and empire's twinge. A century went by and then, Kashtuurlah Rey—the Spanish king—sent bells and a painting of "San José with Child" for the mission church of San Esteban del Rey. The bells were a gift of apology in 1710 for the abduction of the children, as well as for the violence visited upon Acoma in 1599. A king's apology for what Oñate ordered, what Villagrá and his fellow soldiers carried out: massacre, dispersal, children sent to another world. Ortiz writes that in "the south wall / around the graveyard, there is a hole / big enough / for a little boy or little girl to climb through. / They say it is for the Aacqumeh children / who were taken away . . . / to climb through when they return, / Still today the people wait" (70). Acoma will never forgot those children born centuries earlier, nor, as Ortiz writes in the companion poem "Our Children Will Not be Afraid," their children today who link past to present to future and who will be raised "to be wonderful / and healthy, wise and determined against injustice." All these children, spirits and bodies, inhabiting Haak'u and carrying both its burden and joy into another millennium.

Ortiz seizes on a communal will to freedom and defiance against tyranny and violence that is an uncanny echo of Villagrá's Zutacapán, who fictively warned his people that the Spaniards could never be trusted, for they are *ladrones*—thieves. Villagrá speaks through an Acoma when he doubly writes: "to a hard and miserable servitude / I fear we are now doomed and fated. / Is it good that we all together lose / That sweet freedom that was left to us / By those, our ancestors, who came before us? / Take, take up arms and let us await prepared . . . / For it is in our hands to lay them down / If it shall seem best to lay them down" (18.36–53). In "Our Children Will Not Be Afraid," however, Ortiz speaks in his own voice, his own words, not those put into an Acoma character's mouth four centuries earlier:

> Oh shall they, the thieves and killers and liars, endeavor
> to overcome us but will and shall fail. Let their madness
> be their mark; let them fail on their own not from our fears.
> O let them. Let us not flail ourselves upon their illusions . . .

> Our call is for a life that will bring us health,
> a strong and continuous health that wields its spirit
> against those who steal our precious mark
> upon the sacred stone and store of our land . . .
>
> Sing forth then, let all hear from the depths
> of our hungry bones and that marrow that will not dry . . .
>
> Our children will welcome the call and song into their breasts.
> Their dreams will be engendered by Popée, Tecumseh, Crazy Horse,
> Chief Joseph, Geronimo, and all our grandmothers and grandfathers.
> And they will hear them say their lives are our lives, their hearts
> > our hearts.
>
> And they will come to know it will not be the thieves, killers, liars
> but our people who will have victory! (*Out There Somewhere*, 68–69)

The lines here have the effect of sustaining Villagrá's epic curse. The Spaniard cursing himself far into the future through Cotumbo's words here ironically made manifest in a poem by one of the survivors of that January long ago. For Ortiz, victory is situated in memory, the struggles of ancestors: "Popée, Tecumseh, Crazy Horse, Chief Joseph, Geronimo, and all our grandmothers and grandfathers"; in language, safeguarded over the centuries, and that Ortiz made verse in the present; the everyday geometry of land and sky, "the sacred stone and store of our land." History and consciousness rooted in a particular place within the cusp of earth and sky where sits Haakú. The very dirt shifting through his hand defines Acoma's location in time and space. In his poetry, the Keresian language of Haak'u seals home and the future.

I close by asking that we listen to, and learn from, Simon Ortiz's return to his ancient language—from the English translation that accommodates us today in his book of poetry and back to the Keres language that retains all that was and is real in Ortiz, and in Acoma:

Your Life You Are Carrying

This is the dirt
This is the land.

This is ours.
This is our land.

Reach down.
Touch the dirt.
Touch the land.

Pick up the dirt.
Pick up the land.

Dirt you are holding.
Land you are carrying.

Your life you are carrying.
This is what I am showing and telling you.
This is what I am telling and showing you. (*Out There Somewhere*, 90–91)

Kuutra Tsah-tseh-ma Srutai-Kyuiyah

Duwah ya-aie dzah.
Duwah haatse dzah.

Duwah sra-ah.
Duwah sra-ah haatse.

How-nu chuutah.
Pihtya ya-aie
Pihtya haatse.

Dyuu tchu-uh-tah ya-aie.
Dyuu tcha-yow-uuh haatse.

Ya-aie sru-taie-kqui-yah.
Haatse sru-taie-kqui-yah.

Kuutra tsah-tseh-mah sru-taikyuiyah.
Duwaah ehme hau shrauyuu pehni eh sraupeh tah.
Duwaah ehme sraupeh tah eh hau srauyuu pehni.

Notes

Prologue

1. As Rosa Martínez notes, "Publishing in the early seventeenth century required a strenuous censorship process, and manuscripts that disseminated heretical and corrupt philosophies were burned or submitted to the Indexes of prohibited works. As for their creators, they, unfortunately, were persecuted. And so, the interrogation of the *Historia* manuscript lasted four months, and obviously as well as fortunately, the king approved its publication and America's first epic poem was spared from the fires, and the poet from auto de fé." "A Glimpse into the Production and Publication History of the Historia's First Edition" (seminar paper, University of California, Berkeley, 2007), 1.

2. There are three censor approvals: Espinel's quoted above; as well as that of fray Domingo de los Reyes, teacher of divinity and general custos of the Order of Santo Domingo (December 20, 1609), whose approval provides the clerical seal to those recorded a week earlier; and a certain Doctor Cetina, another censor who, it seems, represented the *señores del consejo*, members of the royal council.

3. *La Araucana* was published in three parts, with part one published in 1569, part two in 1578, and part three in 1589. The entire poem then appeared in 1590.

4. Unless otherwise noted, translations are from Miguel Encinas, Alfred Rodríguez, and Joseph P. Sánchez, eds. and trans., *Historia de la Nueva Mexico* (Albuquerque: University of New Mexico Press, 1992).

5. The single best tracing of Villagrá's literary allusions is M. Manuel Martín-Rodríguez's meticulously researched and elegantly argued essay, "'Aquí fue Troia nobles cauallleros': Ecos de la tradición clásica y otros intertextos en la *Historia de la Nueva Mexico*, de Gaspar Pérez de Villagrá," *Silva: Estudios de Humanismo y Tradición Clásica* 4 (2005): 139–208.

6. Encinas, Rodríguez, and Sánchez, *Historia de la Nueva Mexico*, 205.

7. Encinas, Rodríguez, and Sánchez, *Historia de la Nueva Mexico*, 257–58.

8. Part 1, 1569; part 2, 1578; part 3, 1589.

9. As Marc Simmons writes, "A dozen years before, Oñate had marched up this same trail gloriously optimistic and expansive ... Now with a cartload of sobering experiences behind him, he was returning in a very different mood, not defeated perhaps, but certainly chastened, and also a good deal poorer for his efforts. After a brief stopover, we presume, at his home in Zacatecas, he reached Mexico City on April 30, 1610, just a few months short of the fifteen years from the date he had signed his New Mexico contract in the viceregal palace." *The Last Conquistador: Juan de Oñate and the Settling of the Far Southwest* (Norman: University of Oklahoma Press, 1991), 185.

10. "The plain truth was that the colony ... was a shambles and so near to complete disintegration that he found himself compelled to condemn as a traitor anyone who spoke of giving up and returning to the southern provinces. That transformed him from a leader into an oppressor.... In a letter of denunciation addressed to the viceroy and smuggled out of New Mexico at great personal risk, [Captain Velasco] declared that here, 'we are all depressed, cowed, and frightened, expecting death at any moment.'" Simmons, *The Last Conquistador*, 160.

11. *Historia de la Nueva Mexico*, ed. Luis González Obregón, 2 vols. (Mexico City: Imprenta del Museo Nacional, 1900); *Historia de la Nueva Mexico*, ed. Mercedes Junquera (Madrid: Historia 16, 1989); *Historia de la Nueva Mexico*, ed. Miguel Encinas, Alfred Rodríguez, and Joseph P. Sánchez (Albuquerque: University of New Mexico Press, 1992); *Historia de la Nueva Mexico*, ed. Felipe I. Echenique March (Mexico City: Instituto Nacional de Antropología e Historia, Centro Regional de Baja California, 1993).

Gilberto Espinosa offered an excellent prose translation as *A History of New Mexico* in 1933 (Los Angeles: Quivira Society).

Chapter 1

1. See Gonzales's lucid description of the controversy in "'History Hits the Heart': Albuquerque's Great Cuartocentenario Controversy, 1997–2005," in *Expressing New Mexico: Nuevomexicano Creativity, Ritual, and Memory*, ed. Phillip B. Gonzales, 207–32 (Tucson: University of Arizona Press, 2007). See also Kathy Freise's excellent "Contesting Onate: Sculpting the Shape of Memory," 233–54, in the same volume.

2. David Quint offers a different reading of Villagrá that ultimately, I believe, is overly formulaic. The *Historia* reproduces the epic topos of the curse the vanquished issued that Villagrá inherited from the *Aeneid*, the *Pharsalia*, and the *Araucana*; this much Villagrá himself discloses through the allusions to those other poems offered within the poem. Quint, however, relies too heavily on a postcolonial critical template that posits a conscious strategy of closing the poem on an act of suicidal refusal that as much as warns the King that the Indians of la

nueva México will continue to resist Spanish rule; that the Spanish destruction of Acoma was, it turns out, necessary; and that "the Indians are condemned to a future of scattered suicidal gestures, ultimately without aim or direction." David Quint, *Epic and Empire: Politics and Generic Form From Virgil to Milton* (Princeton, NJ: Princeton University Press, 1993), 105. Quint's insistence on this point is based on the assumption that Villagrá's "minor epic," a poem written in "doggerel verse," could not possibly exhibit the kind of intellectual and emotional complexity that would make the final scenes of battle and the destruction of Acoma disclose Villagra's self-doubts about his own role in the assault nor his thinking through of the arrogance and spirit killing nature of empire. What I really want to say about the postcolonial template, though, is that the figure of the "conquistador" is forever stuck in an ideologically ironclad model—a conquistador is a conquistador is a . . . This template will not allow room for internal complexities in a literary work that emerges during empire.

3. George P. Hammond and Agapito Rey, eds., *Don Juan de Oñate, Colonizer of New Mexico, 1595–1628* (Albuquerque: University of New Mexico Press, 1953), 2:1002, 1103, 1007.

4. Hammond and Rey write, "In 1614, Oñate's residencia finally came to a showdown. The government had brought thirty charges against the former governor of New Mexico. . . . Cortés and other conquerors had committed greater misdeeds than Juan de Oñate, but it was his misfortune that there was no great kingdom or other treasure in his province to mitigate the accusations against him. On twelve of the charges he was convicted, of which the chief points were that he had hanged two Indians of Acoma; that he had exercised undue severity in punishing the pueblo of Acoma after it had rebelled; that he had lived an immoral life in the colony; . . . that at his command Captains Villagrá and Márquez had put to death two deserters; that he had reported New Mexico to be a rich and fertile country, while it was really poor and sterile; . . . . that he had delighted in mocking and insulting Juan de Frías Salazar, the royal inspector of his forces." Hammond and Rey, *Don Juan de Oñate, Colonizer*, 1:35.

5. Villagrá opens the *prólogo*: "Una de las mayores infelicidades que puede aver en los hechos humanos es faltarles historiadores, que con sus diligères y catolicas plumas, den vida, conserven y guarden todo quanto la continuacion de los siglos, y flaca memoria de los hombres, consume y deshaze . . . [y] muchos notables varones confieren, diziendo que recibio mayor daño el pueblo Romano en perder lo mucho que de las historias de Ticolivio su coronista nos infalta, que el la declinacion y ruyna de su Imperio, y monarchia que fue la mayor del mundo . . ." (One of the greatest misfortunes in the achievements of a people is to be without historians, who with their quick and universal pens, give life, preserve, and treasure all against the movement of the centuries and the frail memory of men, which wastes away and comes to ruin . . . [And so] many notable men agree, saying that

the Roman people were more endangered by the loss of Titus Livy's histories than of the decline and fall of the empire and the monarchy, which was the greatest in the world [translation mine]).

6. For an interesting essay on Cervantes's commentary on New World events and texts and his own attempts to emigrate to the Americas, see Diana de Armas Wilson's "Cervantes and the New World" in *Cambridge Companion to Cervantes*, ed. Anthony J. Cascardi, 207–8 (New York: Cambridge University Press, 2002).

7. See chapters 47–49 for Cervantes's dramatic dialogue on the literary excesses of his time, whether in the residual popularity of nonsensical books of chivalry or stage plays, which were so bad "actors have to flee and go into hiding."

8. George Parker Winship, ed. and trans., *The Journey of Coronado: 1540–1542* (New York: A. S. Barnes & Company, 1904).

9. Virgil, *The Aeneid*, trans. L. R. Lind (Bloomington: Indiana University Press, 1962).

10. Virgil, *The Aeneid*, trans. Robert Fagles (New York: Viking, 2006).

11. *Historia verdadera de la conquista de la Nueva España* (c. 1568).

12. See José Fernández and Martín Favata, eds. and trans., *The Account: Álvar Núñez Cabeza de Vaca's Relación* (Houston: Arte Público Press, 1993). There are, of course, numerous editions of the Cabeza de Vaca *Relación*, but this more recent edition presents a scholarly annotation to the new translation.

13. See George P. Hammond and Agapito Rey, eds., *Narratives of the Coronado Expedition, 1540–1542* (Albuquerque: University of New Mexico Press, 1940).

14. See F. W. Hodge's foreword in Gaspar Pérez de Villagrá, *A History of New Mexico*, trans. Gilberto Espinosa (Los Angeles: Quivira Society, 1933).

15. Simmons, *The Last Conquistador*, 120.

16. Hammond and Rey, *Don Juan de Oñate, Colonizer*, 2:1111.

17. Quint, *Epic and Empire*. See also José Rabasa, *Writing Violence on the Northern Frontier: The Historiography of Sixteenth-Century New Mexico and Florida and the Legacy of Conquest* (Durham, NC: Duke University Press, 2000). I will take this question up more thoroughly in chapter three.

18. "The Heroic Image in Gaspar de Villagrá's *Historia de la Nueva Mexico*," *The Bilingual Review* 19, no. 1 (1994): 39. Jaramillo's insight into the poem offers a key for understanding Villagrá's subtle irony and political intelligence.

19. Jaramillo, "The Heroic Image," 40.

20. Jaramillo, "The Heroic Image," 46.

21. Villagrá, of course, acknowledges his fascination with hieroglyphics inscribed on stone but notes their difference from European writing. The former script operates at a level of state control, maintaining the record of large social history, dynastic power, sacral narrative, and cosmological knowledge with little space for the personal. The latter, however, provides a space for the intimacy of

diachronic and individual inscription, a letter to a loved one immediately accessible and hence affectively satisfying. Yet this more intimate writing is perishable, the sheet penned to one's wife or children easily destroyed in a house fire, for instance. See canto 1, lines 90–101.

22. In book 6 of the *Pharsalia*, Lucan describes Erictho, the witch Pompey's son Sextus called on to foretell this family's fortune against Caesar. Erictho is viler than the corresponding figure in Villagrá's *Historia*. She consumes the entrails of the dead, opens wombs to eat unborn children, even "drives out the dead and dwells in their tombs." Like Villagrá's maldito, however, Lucan pictures Erictho with:

> Dark matted elf-locks dangling on her brow
> Filthy and foul, a loathsome burden grow;
> Ghastly and frightful-pale her face is seen . . .
> Where-e'er she breathes, blue poison round her spread (821–31)

> And when she speaks
> At length, in murmurs hoarse, her voice was heard
> Her voice, beyond all plants, all magic, feared,
> And by the lowest Stygian gods revered.
> Her gabbling tongue a muttering tone confounds,
> Discordant, and unlike to human sounds:
> It seemed of dogs the bark, of wolves the howl,
> The doleful screeching of the midnight owl,
> The hiss of snakes, the hungry lion's roar,
> The bound of billows beating on the shore (1049–58)

23. Encinas, Rodríguez, and Sánchez, *Historia de la Nueva Mexico*, 7n23.

24. As Elizabeth H. Boone writes, "In the migration histories, Huitzilopochtli either takes an active part in the affairs of the Mexica tribe during the journey from their mythical homeland of Aztlán (Place of the Herons) to Tenochtitlán in the Valley of Mexico or he oversees the activities in a more passive way. . . . In the Codex Boturin, a screenfold of native paper painted in an almost purely Aztec style, Huitzilopochtli's presence on the migration is indicated by a profile with a bird helmet." "Incarnations of the Aztec Supernatural: The Image of Huitzilopochtli in Mexico and Europe," *American Philosophical Society* 79, pt. 2 (1989): 20–21.

25. "New Approaches to Old Chroniclers: Contemporary Critical Theories and the Pérez de Villagrá Epic," in *Recovering the U.S. Hispanic Literary Heritage*, ed. María Herrera-Sobek and Virginia Sánchez-Korrol (Houston: Arte Público, 2000), 3:154–61.

26. Here I am indebted to Richard F. Thomas's discussion of political ambiguity in Virgil. See his "Introduction: The Critical Landscape" for discussion of

the continuing debate on Virgil's critique of Augustus and the Roman Empire in *Virgil and the Augustan Reception* (New York: Cambridge University Press, 2001).

27. Argentina, Venezuela, Chile, Bolivia, Ecuador, Peru, Paraguay, Brazil, Colombia, and Uruguay all declared and fought for their independence during roughly the same period, from 1810 to 1825.

28. Villagrá makes clear that such expeditions were hardly the material of heroic poetry (this notwithstanding Jill Lane's argument that there is nothing "new" in the conquest of New Mexico, all entradas being fully scripted by 1598).

29. The title of hidalgo was promised to those who remained in the King's service for at least five years.

30. Cabeza de Vaca's account was published as *Relación de naufragios y comentarios* in 1542. See Fernández and Favata, *The Account*.

31. "The road-weary Spaniards straggled into Culiacán by early summer [July 1542] with little good to say about the country they had seen . . . The lands which he and his men had traveled held little of interest to a generation of swashbuckling conquistadores—no great cities, no new empire, no signs of gold-and-silver wealth, only cantankerous Indians, whom only the most devoted and saintly missionaries might love, buffalo, prairie dogs, rattlesnakes, burning summers and freezing winters. The veil had been lifted from the 'mystery of the north,' and all were agreed that it might have been better left untouched." John Francis Bannon, writing of the Coronado expedition, in *The Spanish Borderlands Frontier, 1513–1821* (Albuquerque: University of New Mexico Press, 1974), 21.

Chapter 2

1. The fiesta council brochure and the corrido tell us that colonists arrived in July 1598, but the Oñate records show that the main body followed the advance group by a month or more, arriving en masse in late August and celebrating their fiesta in early September.

2. See the league's home page at www.nmhcpl.org.

3. Although I drafted this paragraph before I read Michael L. Trujillo's wonderful "Oñate's Foot: Remembering and Dismembering in Northern New Mexico" (*Aztlan* 33, no. 22 [2008]: 1–119), the resonances are remarkable, especially when Trujillo notes that "the desire for an Oñate icon follows from Nuevomexicanos' struggle to retain their community's integrity. Moreover, this nostalgia is constituted in a discursive field long dominated by Anglo America." He goes on to cite Estevan Arellanos's comment to *New York Times* reporter James Brooke: "When we go to school, we are told that our ancestors came from the East. Well, I don't know of many Martínezes, Arellanos, or Archuletas who had any ancestors who landed at Plymouth Rock" ("Conquistador Statue Stirs Hispanic Pride and Indian Rage," *New York Times*, February 9, 1998, national

edition). As I note in my own recollection above, this is a kind of discursive mantra for Nuevomexicanos, who continue to refuse wholesale assimilation in Anglo America, even though we now speak mostly English and are an integral part of the U.S. consumer society.

4. In 2007, I gave a talk on my Villagrá work at the National Hispanic Cultural Center in Albuquerque. After the talk, a man came up to me at the reception and said, "I think we might be cousins. Tell me who your grandfather was." When I told him, "Melitón Padilla," he said, "Yup, your grandpa and mine are cousins." He then proceeded to tell me he had produced a genealogy showing that our common ancestor was the Esteban noted above and he had published his findings online with the New Mexico Office of the State Historian. Reading that family genealogy on the state historian's website was a fascinating revelation of the complex intermixture of native people and *españoles* throughout New Mexico's Spanish colonial and Mexican periods. In fact, most of the españoles originated in Querétaro, Mexico, where they very likely also already had mestizo roots (New Mexico Office of the State Historian).

5. As Simmons writes in *The Last Conquistador*, 121, Villagrá "joined the Oñate project at its inception and, according to his own statement, invested seven thousand pesos in it, probably the entire sum of his wealth."

6. See settler inventory in George P. Hammond and Agapito Rey, *Narratives of the Coronado Expedition, 1540–1542* (Albuquerque: University of New Mexico Press, 1940), 199–208.

7. *Virgil and the Augustan Reception*, 7–8.

8. See M. Manuel Martín-Rodríguez, "La Historia de la Nueva Mexico de Gaspar Pérez de Villagrá: recepción crítica (con datos biográficos de su autor)," in *El Humanismo Español, Su Proyección en América y Canarias de la Época del Humanismo*, ed. M. Manuel Martín-Rodríguez and Germán Santana Henríquez, 189–253 (Las Palmas: Universidad de Las Palmas de Gran Canaria, 2006).

9. "Record of the Marches by the Army, New Spain to New Mexico, 1596–98," in Hammond and Rey, *Don Juan de Oñate, Colonizer*, 1:309–28, 318.

10. The editors of the *Historia* offer this reference. See 71n5.

11. As Bannon writes in *The Spanish Borderlands Frontier*, 35, Oñate's father, Cristóbal, "was a prominent and wealthy citizen of New Spain, having come to the province in 1524 and having posted an impressive record of long years of service before he became one of the so-called Big Four who opened the silver lodes of Zacatecas—Oñate, Juan de Tolosa, Diego de Ibarra, and Baltasar Treviño."

12. As Encinas, Rodríguez, and Sánchez note in *Historia de la Nueva Mexico*, 131, Farfán's comedia "now lost, would undoubtedly be the first literary work created in what is today the United States."

13. Encinas, Rodríguez, and Sánchez, *Historia de la Nueva Mexico*, 131–32.

14. Encinas, Rodríguez, and Sánchez, *Historia de la Nueva Mexico*, 133.

15. Encinas, Rodríguez, and Sánchez, *Historia de la Nueva Mexico*, 137.
16. Encinas, Rodríguez, and Sánchez, *Historia de la Nueva Mexico*, 134–35.
17. Encinas, Rodríguez, and Sánchez, *Historia de la Nueva Mexico*, 136.
18. All quotations here are from canto fifteen, lines 310–70.
19. Encinas, Rodríguez, and Sánchez, *Historia de la Nueva Mexico*, 131–32.
20. My student Rosa Martínez has detailed just how often ship and seafaring metaphor is at work in Villagrá. As she shows in her summer research project paper (University of California, Berkeley, 2007), Villagrá's trope of desert and vast, open space as ocean is alive in twentieth-century figurations in the narratives of Nuevomexicano writers from Cabeza de Baca's *We Fed Them Cactus* to Rudolfo Anaya's *Bless me, Ultima*.
21. Historian Marc Simmons points out that Oñate had a major uprising on his hands: "Coming only a day or two after arrival of the caravan, its occurrence so early in the game appears all the more puzzling. Involved were forty-five officers and soldiers, more than a third of the expedition's total manpower. They plotted to desert and return to new Spain." Oñate had two captains and a soldier arrested, "identified [them] as ringleaders, and condemned them to death by strangulation." *The Last Conquistador*, 115–16.
22. *Hermanitos Comanchitos: Indo-Hispano Rituals of Captivity and Redemption* (Albuquerque: University of New Mexico Press, 2003), 21.
23. Gutiérrez points out that the Spaniards were performing various enactments of power from the moment they arrived in la nueva México. See *When Jesus Came, the Corn Mothers Went Away: Marriage, Sexuality, and Power in New Mexico, 1500–1846* (Stanford: Stanford University Press, 1991), 46–50. Likewise, Maria O'Malley writes: "Here a performance among the Spanish of 'a jolly drama, well composed / Playing at moors and christians'—one which depicts combativeness—becomes a show of force to exhibit the Spaniards' 'manliness.' Its subject (Spanish aggression toward moors) perpetuates the Spaniards' belief in their superiority over other people. Meanwhile, the natives become afraid through merely watching the drama unfold." "Mapping the Work of Stories in Villagrá's *Historia de la Nueva Mexico*," *Journal of the Southwest* 48, no. 3 (Autumn 2006): 307–30.
24. See Larry Torres, ed. and trans., *Six Nuevomexicano Folk Dramas for Advent Season* (Albuquerque: University of New Mexico Press, 1999), 131.
25. Torres, scene nine, 125.
26. *The Last Conquistador*, 119–20.
27. *Historia de la Nueva Mexico*, 151n3.
28. Simmons writes in *The Last Conquistador*, 121, 123: "Because the young Rodríguez brothers seem to have been his friends, he permitted them to escape although they were the instigators of the horse stealing."
29. As I have already indicated in chapter one, Rabasa argues in *Writing Violence on the Northern Frontier*, 141, that Villagrá wrote the poem "to vindicate Oñate" and "legitimize the war against Acoma."

30. See Alfonso Ortiz, "Ritual Drama and Pueblo World View," and Louis A. Hieb, "Meaning and Mismeaning: Toward an Understanding of the Ritual Clown," in Alfonso Ortiz, ed., *New Perspectives on the Pueblos* (Albuquerque: University of New Mexico Press, 1972). It is, of course, unclear in Villagrá whether the clown figure is a Pueblo man or a Plains Indian, but we do see that the figure who greets the Spaniards as they are making their way on to the Plains is engaged in a burlesque that to this day makes strangers the object of humor or derision. "These range from clown burlesques . . . to mock-Catholic skits such as the mass, baptism, and wedding performed by San Juan clowns each December 26 as part of the Turtle Dance, and rites such as the widespread Sandaro which burlesques and caricatures not only Spaniards but often government officials, missionaries, and tourists." Ortiz, "Ritual Drama," 147.

31. The best studies on the buffalo and the llano are John Miller Morris's *El Llano Estacado: Exploration and Imagination on the High Plains of Texas and New Mexico, 1536–1860* (College Station: Texas State Historical Association, 1997), and Tom McHugh's *The Time of the Buffalo* (New York: Knopf, 1972). Morris and McHugh both astutely trace the first European sightings of the buffalo as they begin with Hernán Cortés, who first sees a buffalo at the palace of Montezuma in 1521, and proceed from the sixteenth to the nineteenth century in the writings of Cabeza de Vaca (1528–32), Gonzalo Fernández de Oviedo y Valdés (1535), Francisco Vásquez de Coronado (1540–42), Pedro de Casteñeda (1540–42), Hernando de Alvarado (1542), Antonio de Espejo (1585), Richard Hakluyt (1589), Samuel Purchas (1613), Thomas Morton (1637), Joliet and Marquette (1673), Daniel Boone (1769), and George Caitlin (1832). In all these accounts, the buffalo are a marvel of massive strength, the odd beauty of their shaggy wool manes and short horns, and their numberless roaming upon the Plains. As Alvarado wrote: "I do not know what to compare them with unless it be the fishes in the sea." The llano, likewise, is described over the centuries as a place of wonder, seemingly unending, flat to the point of monotony except for the waving grass that gives it a vast, shimmering, oceanlike aspect.

32. "Now that I wish to describe the appearance of the bulls, it is to be noticed first that there was not one of the horses that did not take flight when he saw them first, for they have a narrow short face, the brow two palms across from eye to eye, the eyes sticking out at the side, so that, when they are running, they can see who is following them. They have very long beards, like goats, and when they are running they throw their head back with the beard dragging on the ground. There is a sort of girdle round the middle of the body. The hair is very woolly, like a sheep's, very fine, and in front of the girdle the hair is very long and rough like a lion's. They have a great hump, larger than a camel's. The horns are short and thick, so that they are not seen much above the hair. In May, they change the hair in the middle of the body for a down, which makes perfect lions

of them. They rub against the small trees in the little ravines to shed their hair, and they continue this until only the down is left, like a snake changes its skin. They have a short tail, with a bunch of hair at the end. When they run they carry it erect like a scorpion. It is worth noticing that the little calves are red and just like ours, but they change their color and appearance with time and age.... The wool ought to make good cloth on account of its fineness, although the color is not good, because it is the color of buriel [coarse woolen cloth used for making habits for Franciscan friars]. Another thing worth noticing is that the bulls traveled without cows in such large numbers that nobody could have counted them, and so far away from the cows that it was more than 40 leagues from where we began to see the bulls to the place where we began to see the cows. The country they traveled over was so level and smooth that if one looked at them the sky could be seen between their legs, so that if some of them were at a distance they looked like smooth trunked pines whose tops joined, and if there was only one bull it looked as if there were four pines. When one was near them it was impossible to see the ground on the other side of them. The reason for all this was that the country seemed as round as if a man should imagine himself in the three-pint measure, and could see the sky at the edge of it, about a crossbow shot from him, and even if a man only lay down on this back he lost sight of the ground." Winship, *The Journey of Coronado: 1540–1542*, 140–42.

And here is Casteñeda on the Plains people: "People follow the cows, hunting them and tanning the skins to take to the settlements in the winter to sell, since they go there to pass the winter.... These people are called Querechos and Teyas.... They travel like the Arabs, with their tents and troops of dogs loaded with poles and having Moorish pack saddles with girths. When the load gets disarranged, the dogs howl, calling some one to fix them right. These people eat raw flesh. They do not eat human flesh. They are a kind people and not cruel. They are faithful friends. They are able to make themselves very well understood by means of signs." Casteñeda also reports that "They empty a large gut and fill it with blood, and carry this around the neck to drink when they are thirsty. When they open the belly of a cow, they squeeze out the chewed grass and drink the juice that remains behind, because they say that this contains the essence of the stomach." Winship, *The Journey of Coronado: 1540–1542*, 111–12.

Chapter 3

1. Hamilton Tyler, *Pueblo Birds and Myths* (Norman: University of Oklahoma Press, 1979), 17.

2. "Mexican parrots were traditionally raised at Acoma for their beautiful feathers. The parrot and flower design seen here is one of Acoma's most characteristic designs. Among the Pueblo peoples, the color red symbolizes the south

and the parrot designs are usually painted red." Wall plate narrative for exhibition *The Matriarchs*, Haakú Museum.

3. "The move from valley floors to fortified mesa tops during the Kowina phase was almost certainly caused by the appearance of aliens who were a threat to peace. There is no proof that nomadic Athabascans were the culprits. . . . More evidence exists in the Acoma Cultural Province that the aliens were other Puebloans probably displaced by drought, arroyo-cutting, or nomads. . . . if the newcomers were seeking a place to settle they would have been a definite threat to the indigenous population." Reynold J. Ruppé, Jr., *The Acoma Cultural Province: An Archeological Concept* (New York: Garland Press, 1990), 262–63.

4. See Pedro de Castañeda's account of the Coronado expedition in Winship, *The Journey of Coronado: 1540–1542*.

5. Acoma Pueblo website (http://museum.acomaskycity.org/acoma-history), "History of Acoma." Mr. Vallo is no longer director of the cultural center, but people in Acoma regard him highly as the leader of their mission to build the new museum and cultural center.

6. *Great River: The Rio Grande in North American History* (Hanover, NH: Wesleyan University Press, 1984).

7. Ward Alan Minge writes: "Fray Juan is remembered by the Ácomas not only because he ended their isolation from Spanish settlers, but also because he built the large mission church of San Estevan. Those whom Oñate had condemned in 1598 [*sic*; actually 1599] to twenty years of servitude doubtless returned in time to join in one of Ácoma's great historic undertakings—the rebuilding of Old Ácoma. Tradition places responsibility for this task entirely in the hands of Fray Juan." *Ácoma: Pueblo in the Sky*, rev. ed. (Albuquerque: University of New Mexico Press, 2002).

8. The "deliberada fluctuación entre el discurso literario y el historiográfico en su obra la hace salirse de los cánones tradicionalmente asociados con una y otra modalidad discursiva." Indeed, it would be nearly impossible to understand the logic of Martín-Rodríguez's theory of intentional discursive hybridity in a seventeenth-century text without following the consistent fluctuations between poetry and history in the opening twenty cantos over and against the sharp turn to Villagrá's epic rendering of history in the final fourteen cantos that comprise the Acoma battle. Martín-Rodríguez, "La Historia de la Nueva Mexico de Gaspar Pérez de Villagrá: recepción crítica (con nuevos datos biográficos de su autor)," 221.

9. *Writing Violence on the Northern Frontier*, 141.

10. Rabasa, *Writing Violence on the Northern Frontier*, 141.

11. Hammond, *Don Juan de Oñate*, 485–86.

12. Minge, *Ácoma: Pueblo in the Sky*, 15.

13. Robert Fitzgerald writes in the postscript to his translation of the *Aeneid* that the recent warfare between the Carthaginian general Hannibal would have

been immediately in the minds of readers when Aeneas narrowly escapes from Dido's Carthage. "Dido indeed in her final curse called for future strife without quarter between her descendents and those of Aeneas and prayed for one Carthaginian in particular, aliquis ultor, 'someone to avenge me.' At this the Roman reader murmured 'Hannibal.'" Virgil, *The Aeneid* (New York: Vintage, 1990), 406.

14. Minge, *Ácoma: Pueblo in the Sky*, 11.

15. Smith notes that the "ultimate source" for such speech is to be found in Herodotus, "who never fails to give direct voices to the alien peoples whose history he records, including the Greeks' great enemy, the Persians" and Thucydides, where he counts 141 formal orations in the *Peloponnesian Wars*, which are generally "orations of generals to their armies and debates before battle, both of which serve to show the inner workings of the speakers' minds." In other words, Smith implicitly concedes that literary and historiographic speech is, and always has been, an invented artifact. "Mouthpieces: Native American Voices in Thomas Harriot's *True and Brief Report of . . . Virginia*, Gaspar Pérez de Villagrá's *Historia de la Nueva Mexico*, and John Smith's *General History of Virginia*," *New Literary History* 32 (Summer 2001): 511.

16. Williams writes: "While we must agree that the Roman vision was one theme of the poem, indeed the principal and dominant one (though not necessarily the most important), there are other themes against which the implications of the Roman theme are explored. We might call the Roman element Virgil's public voice, if we may do so without implying that it was feigned in any way—for it was not; how shall we define the private voice of the poet? We associate it most strongly with Dido and the apparently senseless suffering of her tragedy; and with Turnus who does what he thinks is right and loses his life . . . and the countless warriors who fall in battle . . ." "The Purpose of the *Aeneid*," in *Oxford Readings in Vergil's Aeneid*, ed. S. J. Harrison (New York: Oxford University Press, 1990), 25.

17. Hammond and Rey, *Don Juan de Oñate, Colonizer*, 1:428–79.

18. Hammond and Rey, *Don Juan de Oñate, Colonizer*, 1:429.

19. See the "Act of Obedience and Vassalage by the Indians of Acoma" in Hammond and Rey, *Don Juan de Oñate, Colonizer*, 1:354–56. The act was a template statement Oñate made to each pueblo, telling them that "he had come to their country to bring them to the knowledge of God and the king. . . . and it was fitting that they render obedience and vassalage to God and the king." As the Spanish scribe reports, on October 27, 1598, the Acoma rendered their obedience: "The chieftains, having heard and understood the above and conferred among themselves . . . replied with spontaneous signs of pleasure and accord that they wished to become vassals."

20. Hammond and Rey, *Don Juan de Oñate, Colonizer*, 1:446.

21. Hammond and Rey, *Don Juan de Oñate, Colonizer*, 1:445–46.

22. Hammond and Rey, *Don Juan de Oñate, Colonizer*, 1:463.

23. Hammond and Rey, *Don Juan de Oñate, Colonizer,* 1:449. Also see similar reference in the letter of "Alfonso Sanchez to Rodrigo del Rio, February 28, 1599": "At this time there arose a minor incident when a solder named Vivero took two turkeys from the Indians and they killed him from one of the terraces. The entire pueblo then rose in arms and killed the maese de campo . . ." Hammond and Rey, *Don Juan de Oñate, Colonizer,* 1:426.

24. Hammond and Rey, *Don Juan de Oñate, Colonizer,* 1:471.

25. Hammond and Rey, *Don Juan de Oñate, Colonizer,* 1:474.

26. Hammond and Rey, *Don Juan de Oñate, Colonizer,* 1:467.

27. Hammond and Rey, *Don Juan de Oñate, Colonizer,* 1:466.

28. Hammond and Rey, *Don Juan de Oñate, Colonizer,* 1:466.

29. For Laertius, see Encinas, Rodríguez, and Sánchez's editorial note, *Historia de la Nueva Mexico,* 211.

30. "Testimony of Antonio de Sariñana," Hammond and Rey, *Don Juan de Oñate, Colonizer,* 1:450.

31. Hammond and Rey, *Don Juan de Oñate, Colonizer,* 1:447.

32. See Rabasa, *Writing Violence on the Northern Frontier,* 142.

33. Gaspar Pérez de Villagrá, *Historia de la Nueva Mexico* (Alcalá de Henares: Luis Martínez Grande, 1610), 222.

34. "Clearly, Villagrá seeks to vindicate Oñate and all those who participated in the massacre at Acoma. His epic poem aspires to be a monumental history that would preserve the memory of the deeds of those who entered Nuevo México to conquer and convert its people." Rabasa, *Writing Violence on the Northern Frontier,* 141.

35. Letter of fray Alonso Martínez, comisario apostólico, in Encinas, Rodríguez, and Sánchez, *Historia de la Nueva Mexico,* 222–24. See also Hammond and Rey, *Don Juan de Oñate, Colonizer,* 1:451–54.

36. Oñate then orders Vicente de Zaldívar, the commander of the force: "You will arrest all of the people, young and old, without sparing anyone . . . you will punish all those of fighting age as you deem best, as a warning to everyone in the kingdom . . . those you execute you will expose to public view at the places you think most suitable, as a salutary example." Hammond and Rey, *Don Juan de Oñate, Colonizer,* 1:458–59.

37. Smith, "Mouthpieces: Native American Voices," 513.

38. Hammond and Rey, *Don Juan de Oñate, Colonizer,* 1:470.

39. Encinas, Rodríguez, and Sánchez, *Historia de la Nueva Mexico,* 252n1.

40. *The Spanish Frontier in North America* (New Haven, CT: Yale University Press, 1992), 86.

41. Hammond and Rey, *Don Juan de Oñate, Colonizer,* 1:438.

42. *The Spanish Frontier in North America,* 86.

43. Weber, *The Spanish Frontier in North America,* 86.

44. Quint, *Epic and Empire,* 105.

45. Quint, *Epic and Empire*, 105.

46. See Michael L. Trujillo's excellent study of the complex politics of the "historical reconstruction of 'Spanish' icons in northern New Mexico" and the "removal of the Oñate statue's foot" as retribution for the "brutal colonial encounter in 1599" in "Oñate's Foot," 91–119.

Epilogue

1. Hammond and Rey, *Don Juan de Oñate, Colonizer*, 1:477–78.

2. All the poems cited here are from Simon J. Ortiz's *Out There Somewhere* (Tucson: University of Arizona Press, 2002).

3. The speaker locates himself in different parts of the world where Indians are dealing with displacements, "just like always." In Martinique, Ortiz recalls being told that there is a "magic-mystic tree ... that never dies. / It's called Acoma, exactly like you spell Acoma." The magic-mystic tree and Acoma, the writer's pueblo, are symbolically linked by global threats to indigenous people against their unremitting will to survive.

Bibliography

Arteaga, Alfred. *Chicano Poetics: Heterotexts and Hybrídíties*. New York: Cambridge University Press, 1997.

Bannon, John Francis. *The Spanish Borderlands Frontier, 1513–1821*. Albuquerque: University of New Mexico Press, 1974.

Bodmer, Beatriz Pastor. *The Armature of Conquest: Spanish Accounts of the Discovery of America, 1492–1589*. Stanford: Stanford University Press, 1992.

Bolton, Hubert E. *Spanish Exploration in the Southwest, 1542–1706*. New York: Charles Scribner's Sons, 1925.

Boone, Elizabeth H. *Incarnations of the Aztec Supernatural: The Image of Huitzilopochtli in Mexico and Europe*. Transactions of the American Philosophical Society 79, kpt. 2. Philadelphia: American Philosophical Society, 1989.

Bustamante, Adrian. "'The Matter was Never Resolved': The *Casta* System in Colonial New Mexico, 1693–1823." *New Mexico Historical Review* 66, no. 2 (April 1991): 143–63.

Camões, Luís Vaz de. *The Lusiads*. Translated by William C. Atkinson. New York: Penguin, 1952.

El Capitan Gaspar de Villagrá, para justificación de las muertes, justicias, y castigos que el Adelantado don Juan de Oñate dizen que hizo en Nueva Mexico, 1612. Madrid, 1612.

Chávez, Thomas E. *New Mexico: Past and Future*. Albuquerque: University of New Mexico Press, 2006.

Cornish, Beatrice Quijada. "The Ancestry and Family of Juan de Oñate." In *The Pacific Ocean in History*, edited by H. Morse Stephens and Herbert E. Bolton, 452–66. New York: The MacMillan Co., 1917.

Cowans, Jon, ed. *Early Modern Spain: A Documentary History*. Philadelphia: University of Pennsylvania Press, 2003.

Crespo-Francés y Valero, José Antonio. *La Expedición de Juan de Oñate*. Madrid: Soutuer Ediciones, 1997.

Cruickshank, D. W. "'Literature' and the Book Trade in Golden-Age Spain." *The Modern Language Review* 73, no. 4 (October, 1978): 799–824.

Díaz del Castillo, Bernal. *Historia verdadera de la conquista de la Nueva España: Manuscrito "Guatemala."* Edición Crítica de José Antonio Barbón Rodríguez. Mexico City: Colegio de México/Universidad Nacional Autónoma de México, 2005.

———. *The True History of the Conquest of Mexico (1568)*. Translated by Maurice Keating. London: George G. Harrap, 1928.

Dillingham, Rick. *Acoma and Laguna Pottery*. Santa Fe: School of American Research, 1992.

Ercilla, Alonso de. *La Araucana*. Santiago, Chile: Empresa Editora, 1958.

Espinosa, J. Manuel, ed. *The Pueblo Indian Revolt of 1696, and the Franciscan Missions in New Mexico: Letters of the Missionaries and Related Documents*. Norman: University of Oklahoma Press, 1988.

Fernández-Armesto, Felipe. *Pathfinders: A Global History of Exploration*. New York: W. W. Norton, 2006.

Fernández, José, and Martín Favata, eds. and trans. *The Account: Álvar Núñez Cabeza de Vaca's Relación*. Houston: Arte Público Press, 1993.

Freise, Kathy. "Contesting Oñate: Sculpting the Shape of Memory." In *Expressing New Mexico: Nuevomexicano Creativity, Ritual, and Memory*, edited by Phillip B. Gonzales, 233–54. Tucson: University of Arizona Press, 2007.

García-Mason, Velma. "Acoma Pueblo." In *Handbook of North American Indians*, edited by Alfonso Ortiz, 9:450–66. Washington, DC: Smithsonian, 1979.

Gonzales, Phillip B. *Expressing New Mexico: Nuevomexicano Creativity, Ritual, and Memory*. Tucson: University of Arizona Press, 2007.

———. "'History Hits the Heart': Albuquerque's Great Cuartocentario Controversy, 1997–2005." In *Expressing New Mexico: Nuevomexicano Creativity, Ritual, and Memory*, edited by Phillip B. Gonzales, 207–32. Tucson: University of Arizona Press, 2007.

Gonzales-Berry, Erlinda. *Pasó Por Aquí: Critical Essays on the New Mexico Literary Tradition, 1542–1988*. Albuquerque: University of New Mexico Press, 1989.

Grafton, Anthony. *New Worlds, Ancient Texts: The Power of Tradition and the Shock of Discovery*. Cambridge, MA: Harvard University Press, 1992.

Greenblatt, Stephen. *Marvelous Possessions: The Wonder of the New World*. Chicago: University of Chicago Press. 1991.

Greenblatt, Stephen, ed. *New World Encounters*. Berkeley: University of California Press, 1993.

Gunn, John M. *Shat-Chen: History, Traditions and Narratives of the Queres Indians of Laguna and Acoma*. Albuquerque: Albright and Anderson, 1917.

Gutiérrez, Ramón A. *When Jesus Came, the Corn Mothers Went Away: Marriage, Sexuality, and Power in New Mexico, 1500–1846*. Stanford: Stanford University Press, 1991.

Hammond, George P. *Don Juan de Oñate and the Founding of New Mexico, 1595–1620*. Santa Fe: El Palacio Press, 1927.

Hammond, George P., and Agapito Rey, eds. *Don Juan de Oñate, Colonizer of New Mexico, 1595–1628*. 2 vols. Albuquerque: University of New Mexico Press, 1953.

———. *Narratives of the Coronado Expedition, 1540–1542*. Albuquerque: University of New Mexico Press, 1940.

Harrison, S. J., ed. *Oxford Readings in Vergil's Aeneid*. New York: Oxford University Press, 1990.

Herrera-Sobek, María. "Gaspar Pérez de Villagrá's Memorial: Aristotelian Rhetoric and the Discourse of Justification in a Colonial Genre." *Genre* 31, no.12 (Spring–Summer 1999): 85–98.

———. "The Homeric Image in Gaspar de Villagrá's *Historia de la Nueva México.*" *Bilingual Review/La Revista Bilingüe* 23, no. 2 (May–August 1998): 137–44.

———. "New Approaches to Old Chroniclers: Contemporary Critical Theories and the Pérez de Villagrá Epic." In *Recovering the U.S. Hispanic Literary Heritage*, edited by María Herrera-Sobek, and Virginia Sánchez-Korrol, 3:154–62. Houston: Arte Público Press, 2000.

———. *Reconstructing a Chicano/a Literary Heritage*. Tucson: University of Arizona Press, 1993.

Highet, Gilbert. *The Speeches of Virgil*. Princeton, NJ: Princeton University Press, 1972.

Homer. *The Odyssey*. Translated by Robert Fagles. New York: Penguin, 1996.

Horgan, Paul. *Great River: The Rio Grande in North American History*. Hanover, NH: Wesleyan University Press, 1955.

Jaramillo, Philadelphio. "The Heroic Image in Gaspar de Villagrá's *Historia de la Nueva Mexico*." *The Bilingual Review* 19, no. 1 (1994): 39–47.

———. *Historia de Nueva México del Capitán Gaspar Pérez de Villagrá; edición paleográfica, con notas y estudio preliminar*. PhD diss., New Mexico State University, 1990.

Kamen, Henry. *Empire: How Spain Became a World Power, 1492–1763*. New York: Perennial, 2003.

Kessell, John L. *Pueblos, Spaniards and the Kingdom of New Mexico*. Norman: University of Oklahoma, 2008.

———. *Spain in the Southwest*. Norman: University of Oklahoma Press, 2002.

Knapp, Jeffrey. *An Empire Nowhere: England, America and Literature from Utopia to The Tempest*. Berkeley: University of California Press, 1992.

Lamadrid, Enrique R. *Hermanitos Comanchitos: Indo-Hispano Rituals of Captivity and Redemption*. Albuquerque: University of New Mexico Press, 2003.

Lane, Jill. "On Colonial Forgetting: The Conquest of New Mexico and its *Historia*." In *The Ends of Performance*, edited by Peggy Phelan and Jill Lane, 52–69. New York: New York University Press, 1988.

Las Casas, Bartolomé de. *The Short Account of the Destruction of the Indies*. Translated and edited by Nigel Griffin. New York: Penguin, 1992.

Leal, Luis. "The First American Epic: Villagrá's History of New Mexico." In *Pasó Por Aquí: Critical Essays on the New Mexican Literary Tradition, 1542–1988*, edited by Erlinda Gonzales-Berry, 47–62. Albuquerque: University of New Mexico Press, 1989.

———. "Poetic Discourse in Pérez de Villagrá's *Historia de la Nueva Mexico*." In *Reconstructing a Chicano/a Literary Heritage*, edited by María Herrera-Sobek, 95–117. Tucson: University of Arizona Press, 1993.

León-Portilla, Miguel. *Aztec Thought and Culture: A Study of the Ancient Nahuatl Mind*. Translated by Jack Emory Davis. Norman: University of Oklahoma Press, 1963.

Lomelí, Francisco A., Victor A. Sorell, and Genaro M. Padilla, eds. *Nuevomexicano Cultural Legacy: Forms, Agencies, and Discourse*. Albuquerque: University of New Mexico Press. 2002.

López, Miguel. "Disputed History and Poetry: Gaspar Pérez de Villagrá's *Historia de la Nueva Mexico.*" *Bilingual Review* 26, no.1 (January–April): 43–56.

Lucan. *Pharsalia: The Civil War.* Edited by Sarah Brown and Charles Martindale. Translated by Nicholas Rowe. London: Everyman, 1998.

Lyne, R. O. A. M. "Virgil and the Politics of War." In *Oxford Readings in Vergil's Aeneid*, edited by S. J. Harrison, 316–38. Oxford: Oxford University Press, 1990.

Martín-Rodríguez, M. Manuel. "'Aquí fue Troia nobles cauallleros': Ecos de la tradición clásica y otros intertextuales en la *Historia de la Nueva Mexico*, de Gaspar Pérez de Villagrá." *Silva: Estudios de Humanismo y Tradición Clásica* 4 (2005): 139–208.

———. "La Historia de la Nueva Mexico de Gaspar Pérez de Villagrá: recepción crítica (con nuevos datos biográficos de su autor)." In *El Humanismo Español, Su Proyección en América y Canarias de la Época del Humanismo*, edited by M. Manuel Martín-Rodríguez and Germán Santana Henríquez, 189–253. Las Palmas: Universidad de Las Palmas de Gran Canaria, 2006.

———. *Gaspar de Villagrá: Legista, Soldado y Poeta.* León: Universidad de León, 2009.

Martínez, Rosa. "A Glimpse into the Production and Publication History of the *Historia*'s First Edition." Seminar paper, University of California, Berkeley, October 2007.

———. "*Libras tu del olvido*": Gaspar Pérez de Villagrá's *Historia de la Nueva Mexico* (1610). Paper, summer research project, University of California, Berkeley, 2006.

McHugh, Tom. *The Time of the Buffalo.* New York: Knopf, 1972.

Minge, Ward Alan. *Ácoma: Pueblo in the Sky.* Rev. ed. Albuquerque: University of New Mexico Press, 2002.

Montoya, Juan de. *New Mexico in 1602.* Translated by George P. Hammond and Agapito Rey. Albuquerque: Quivira Society, 1938.

Morris, John Miller. *El Llano Estacado: Exploration and Imagination on the High Plains of Texas and New Mexico, 1536–1860.* College Station: Texas State Historical Association, 1997.

Murrin, Michael. *History and Warfare in Renaissance Epic.* Chicago: University of Chicago Press, 1994.

O'Malley, Maria. "Mapping the Work of Stories in Villagrá's *Historia de la Nueva Mexico.*" *Journal of the Southwest* 48, no. 3 (Autumn 2006): 307–30.

Ortiz, Alfonso, ed. *New Perspectives on the Pueblos.* Albuquerque: University of New Mexico Press, 1972.

Ortiz, Simon. *Out There Somewhere.* Tucson: University of Arizona Press, 2002.

———. *Woven Stone.* Tucson: University of Arizona Press, 1992.

Padilla, Genaro M. "Discontinuous Continuities: Remapping the Terrain of Spanish Colonial Narrative." In *Reconstructing a Chicano/a Literary Heritage*, edited by María Herrera-Sobek, 24–36. Tucson: University of Arizona Press. 1993.

Pérez-Linggi, Sandra M. "Gaspar Pérez de Villagrá: *Criollo* or Chicano in the Southwest?" *Hispania* 88, no. 4 (2005): 666–76.

Phillips, Christopher N. "Lighting Out for the Rough Ground: America's Epic Origins and the Richness of World Literature." *Proceedings of the Modern Languages Association* 122, no. 5 (October 2007): 1499–1515.

Quint, David. *Epic and Empire: Politics and Generic Form From Virgil to Milton*. Princeton, NJ: Princeton University Press, 1993.

Rabasa, José. *Writing Violence on the Northern Frontier: The Historiography of Sixteenth-Century New Mexico and Florida and the Legacy of Conquest*. Durham, NC: Duke University Press, 2000.

Ruppé, Reynold J., Jr. *The Acoma Cultural Province: An Archeological Concept*. New York: Garland Press, 1990.

Sando, Joe S. *Pueblo Nations: Eight Centuries of Pueblo Indian History*. Santa Fe: Clear Light Publishers, 1992.

———, and Herman Agoyo. *Po'Pay: Leader of the First American Revolution*. Santa Fe: Clear Light Publishing, 2005.

Schmidt-Nowara, Christopher, and John M. Nieto-Phillips, eds. *Interpreting Spanish Colonialism: Empires, Nations, and Legends*. Albuquerque: University of New Mexico Press, 2005.

Sedgwick, Mrs. William T. *Acoma, the Sky City: A Study in the Pueblo-Indian History and Civilization*. Cambridge, MA: Harvard University Press, 1926.

Shea, John Gilmary. "The First Epic of our Country. By the Poet Conquistador of New Mexico, Captain Gaspar de Villagrá." New York: United States Historical Society, 1887.

Sider, Sandra. *Handbook to Life in Renaissance Europe*. New York: Oxford University Press, 2005.

Simmons, Marc. *The Last Conquistador: Juan de Oñate and the Settling of the Far Southwest*. Norman: University of Oklahoma Press, 1991.

Smith, Bruce R. "Mouthpieces: Native American Voices in Thomas Harriot's *True and Brief Report of . . . Virginia*, Gaspar Pérez de Villagrá's *Historia de la Nueva Mexico*, and John Smith's *General History of Virginia*." *New Literary History* 32 (Summer 2001): 501–17.

Strauss, Barry. *The Trojan War: A New History*. New York: Simon and Schuster, 2006.

Thomas, Richard F. *Virgil and the Augustan Reception*. New York: Cambridge University Press, 2001.

Torres, Larry, ed. and trans. *Six Nuevomexicano Folk Dramas for the Advent Season*. Albuquerque: University of New Mexico Press, 1999.

Trujillo, Michael L. "Oñate's Foot: Remembering and Dismembering in Northern New Mexico." *Aztlan* 33, no. 22 (2008): 91–119.

Tyler, Hamilton. *Pueblo Birds and Myths*. Norman: University of Oklahoma Press, 1979.

Vázquez, Dizán. "Gaspar Pérez de Villagrá: cronista de Chihuahua en su *Historia de Nuevo México*." *Boletín UEHS* 48 (November 2006).

Villagrá, Gaspar Pérez de. *Historia de la Nueva Mexico*. Alcalá de Henares: Luis Martínez Grande, 1610.

———. *Historia de la Nueva Mexico*. Edited by Felipe I. Echenique March. Mexico City: Instituto Nacional de Antropología e Historia, Centro Regional de Baja California, 1993.

———. *Historia de la Nueva Mexico*. Edited and translated by Miguel Encinas, Alfred Rodríguez, and Joseph P. Sánchez. Albuquerque: University of New Mexico Press, 1992.

———. *Historia de la Nueva Mexico.* Edited by Luis González Obregón. 2 vols. Mexico City: Imprenta del Museo Nacional, 1900.
———. *Historia de la Nueva Mexico.* Edited by Mercedes Junquera. Madrid: Historia 16, 1989.
———. *A History of New Mexico.* Translated by Gilberto Espinosa. Los Angeles: Quivira Society, 1933.
Virgil. *The Aeneid.* Translated by Robert Fagles. New York: Viking, 2006.
———. *The Aeneid.* Translated by Robert Fitzgerald. New York: Vintage, 1990.
———. *The Aeneid.* Translated by L. R. Lind. Bloomington: Indiana University Press, 1962.
Weber, David J. *Myth and the History of the Hispanic Southwest.* Albuquerque: University of New Mexico Press, 1988.
———. *The Spanish Frontier in North America.* New Haven, CT: Yale University Press, 1992.
Williams, R. D. "The Purpose of the *Aeneid*." In *Oxford Readings in Vergil's Aeneid*, edited by S. J. Harrison, 21–36. New York: Oxford University Press, 1990.
Wilson, Diana de Armas. "Cervantes and the New World." In *Cambridge Companion to Cervantes*, edited by Anthony J. Cascardi, 207–8. New York: Cambridge University Press, 2002.
Winship, George Parker, ed. and trans. *The Journey of Coronado: 1540–1542.* New York: A. S. Barnes & Company, 1904.
Wogan, Daniel. "Ercilla y la poesía mexicana." *Revista Iberoamericana* 3, no. 6 (May 1941): 371–79.

Index

Acoma: Church of San Estevan, 87, 88, 122, 128, 141n7; contemporary, 122–23; expedition to, 14; Haakú Museum, 83–84, 140–41n2; land of, 87; massacre at, 100–101, 119–21, 125–28; Ohkay Owingeh and, 67; Oñate and, 22–23, 93; Oñate sentence against, 119–20, 126–27, 127–29, 141n7; pottery of, 43–45, 140–41n2; Sky City, 23, 83, 86
Aeneid, 3, 6, 18, 19, 22, 38, 73, 89, 91, 109, 132n2, 141–42n13
Albuquerque Museum, 11, 42, 46
Alurista, 37
Alvarado, Hernando de, 139n31
Amadis of Gaul, 19
Anaya, Rudolfo A., 37, 138n20
Annals, 57
Apaches, 78, 79–80
Araucana, La, 3, 5, 9, 16, 19, 25, 93, 131n3, 132n2
Arellanos, Estevan, 136–37n3
Aztecs, 7, 27–35, 37–38, 73, 85
Aztlán: Essays on the Chicano Homeland, 37

Bannon, Francis, 136n31, 137n11
Blázquez de Cabanillas, Juan, 102–3
Bless Me, Ultima, 37, 138n20
Bolton, Herbert, 20–21
Boone, Elizabeth H., 135n24
Brevísima relación de la destrucción de las Indias, 97

Cabeza de Baca, Fabiola, 138n20

Cabeza de Vaca, Alvar Nuñez, 18, 20, 39–40, 79, 136n30, 139n31
Camões, Luís Vaz de, 7, 27, 38
Casas, Bartolomé de las, 97
Casteñeda de Nájera, Pedro, 20, 78, 140n32, 141n4
Cervantes, Miguel de, 4, 16–19, 39, 134n6, 134n7; *Don Quixote,* 5, 17–18; *El cerco de Numancia,* 17, 19
Chamuscada, Francisco, 40
Chicanos, 37, 45, 48–50, 86, 88
Coronado, Francisco de, 40, 64, 74, 75, 78, 79, 85, 136n31
"Corrido de Juan de Oñate, El," 43–44, 45, 48–49
Cortés, Hernán, 40, 68, 96–97, 133n4, 139n31

Díaz del Castillo, Bernal, 20, 99
Don Juan de Oñate, Colonizer of New Mexico, 1595–1628, 56
Durán, Diego de, 32

Echenique, Felipe I., 132n11
Encinas, Miguel, 70, 131n4, 132n11, 137n10, 137n12
Ercilla, Alonso de, 3, 5, 9, 16, 19, 22, 25, 30, 93, 97
Española, 45, 47
Española Fiesta, 45, 48–49, 53, 88, 136n1
Espejo, Antonio de, 40, 79, 139n31
Espinel, Vicente, 20
Espinosa, Gilbert, 132n11

Favata, Martín, 134n12

Felipe II, 17
Felipe III, 7, 14, 26, 28, 36, 39, 40, 42, 92
Fernández, José, 134n12
Fernández de Oviedo y Valdés, Gonzalo, 139n31
Floricanto en Aztlán, 37
Freise, Kathy, 132n1

Gonzales, Phillip B., 11, 132n1
Great River, 86
Gutiérrez, Ramón A., 66, 138n32
Guzmán, Saavedra, 16

Hammond, George P., 22, 56, 133n4, 134n13, 137n6, 142n19, 143n23
Heart of Aztlán, 37
hermosa Ester, La, 1
Herodotus, 110
Herrera-Sobek, María, 35
Historia de la benida de los indios, 31
Historia de la Nueva Mexico: "Act of Possession" in, 58–60, 62–63; Aztec empire in, 7, 27–35, 37–38, 73; battle at Acoma, 110–14; common soldiers in, 8, 57, 70–72, 112–14; critiques King and court, 42; dedicated to Felipe III, 36; massacre at Acoma in, 80–81, 90–6, 101–7, 108, 109, 115–19; material book, 2–5; mestizaje in, 35–36; *Moros y Cristianos* in, 66–68; native people in, 60–62, 64; Oñate in, 7–8, 24–26, 29, 40–42, 46–48, 57–60, 62, 68, 113–14; Plains people in, 73–80; publication history, 10, 30, 31–32; quotes official archive, 21–23, 56–57, 107–8; reception of, 5; settlers in, 39, 81–82; use of Virgil's *Aeneid* in, 6–8, 19, 24–26, 65, 89, 91–94, 96, 97, 104; Villagrá portrait in, 18
Historia de la Nueva Mexico, Del Capitán Gaspar de Villagrá. See *Historia de la Nueva Mexico*
Historia de las Indias de Nueva España, 32
Historia general de México, 31–32
Hodge, F. W., 134n14
Homer, 3, 6, 16, 19, 22, 24, 31, 40, 73, 91, 92, 101, 114, 116, 119
Hopi, 81

Horgan, Paul, 86
Iliad, The, 22, 73, 76, 91, 119
Institutio Oratoria, 36

Jaramillo, Philadelphio, 25–26, 134n18
Junquera, Mercedes, 132n11

Lamadrid, Enrique R., 66
Lane, Jill, 136n28
Laso de la Vega, Francisco, 16
Last Conquistador: Juan de Oñate and the Settling of the Far Southwest, The, 21, 132n9, 132n10, 138n28
La Villa Real de la Santa Fe de San Francisco de Asís. See Santa Fe
Livy, Titus, 6, 16, 56, 57
Llano Estacado, 73
Lomelí, Francisco A., 37
Lope de Vega, Félix Arturo: *La hermosa Ester*, 1; *Péribáñez*, 1
Lucan, 6, 16, 31, 35, 132n2, 135n22

Machu Picchu, 68
Martínez, Rosa, 131n1, 138n20
Martin-Rodriguez, M. Manuel, 55, 89, 131n5, 137n8, 141n8
McHugh, Tom, 139n31
mestizaje, 45, 49, 50, 54
Metamorphoses, 6, 119
Mexicana, 16
Mexico, 34, 37
Minge, Ward Alan, 141n7
Moros y Cristianos, 66, 70, 74, 88, 112
Morris, John Miller, 139n31

New Mexico Hispanic Cultural Preservation League, 49, 88, 96, 122, 136n2

Obregón, Luis González, 20, 132n11
Odyssey, The, 19
Ohkay Owingeh, 5, 12, 27, 45, 46, 47–48, 51–53, 63, 65, 69, 75, 109, 122; *Moros y Cristianos* at, 66, 68
O'Malley, Maria, 138n23
Oñate, Juan de: charged with war crimes, 15, 89, 90, 119; conviction of, 22, 53, 121; Española celebration of, 88;

family of, 58, 137n11; imposes "Act of Obedience," 93, 142n19; leads colonial expedition, 3, 6, 15, 18, 38, 47, 55, 81, 82, 136n1; orders execution of deserters, 69, 70, 71; orders war at Acoma, 107–8; representation in statuary, 11–12, 27, 122; resigns as governor, 9; sentence against Acoma, 119–20; trial of Acoma survivors, 91, 107
Ortiz, Alfonso, 139n30
Ortiz, Simon J., 125–26, 127–30, 144n3
Os Lusiadas, 7, 27
Out There Somewhere, 127–30
Ovid, 6, 119

Padilla, Esperanza, 50, 51–52, 125–26, 127
Parallel Lives, 57
Peralta, Pedro de, 9
peregrino indiano, El, 16
Pharsalia, 6, 16, 35, 132n2, 135n22
Pizarro, Francisco, 68
Plutarch, 57
Po'pay, 122
Primeros memoriales, 32
Pueblo Revolt, 53, 88, 108, 122

Quint, David, 22–23, 120, 122, 132–33n2
Quintilian, 6, 36
Quintillius, 55

Rabasa, José, 89–90, 99, 107, 134n17, 138n29, 143n34
Rael-Gálvez, Estevan, 137n4
Ramírez, Fray Juan, 87, 122, 141n7
Relación, 20, 79
Rey, Agapito, 56, 133n4, 134n13, 137n6, 142n19, 143n23
Rodríguez, Alfred, 70, 131n4, 132n11, 137n10, 137n12
Ruppé, Reynold J. Jr., 141n3

Sahagún, Bernardino de, 31–32, 35
Sánchez, Joseph P., 131n4, 132n11, 137n10, 137n12

San Gabriel. *See* Yunque Yunque
San Juan. *See* Ohkay Owingeh
Santa Fe, 2, 9
Santo Domingo Pueblo, 23, 61–62
Seneca, 6
Simmons, Marc, 21, 70, 132n9, 132n10, 137n5, 138n21, 138n28
Sky City. *See* Acoma
Smith, Bruce R., 94, 99, 110, 142n15

Tenochtitlán, 12, 9–20, 27, 28, 32–34, 55, 68, 97
Thomas, Richard, 55, 135–36n26
Thucydides, 110
Torquatus, 69, 70
Torres, Larry, 138n24
Tovar, Juan de, 31
Trujillo, Michael L., 136–37n3, 144n46

Vallo, Brian, 86, 141n5
Vasco de Gama expedition, 7, 27
Vasquez de Coronado, Francisco, 15
Villagrá, Gaspar Pérez de: birth, 1; charged with war crimes, 72, 89, 90; convicted of war crimes, 121; as criollo, 34–37, 80; death, 9–10; dedicates work to Felipe III, 7; education of, 6, 15–16, 58, 91, 107; leaves Oñate expedition, 71–72, 121; in Mexico, 14, 15; participant in Acoma massacre, 103–4; as soldier, 47; writes "Justification," 69, 72
Virgil, 16, 18, 19, 22, 38, 55, 65, 73, 89, 97, 98–99, 101, 109, 116, 119, 135–36n26

Weber, David J., 115, 119, 120
We Fed Them Cactus, 138n20
Williams, R. D., 98, 142n16
Wilson, Diana de Armas, 134n6
Winship, George Parker, 139–40n32

Yunque Yunque, 2, 9

Zuni, 81